Revised Edition

12.95 4.88

Discovering the
California
Coast

Discovering the
California

A Sunset Pictorial

Coast

LANE PUBLISHING CO., MENLO PARK, CALIFORNIA

Edited by JACK MCDOWELL

Design Consultant: Cummings Walker
Maps and Lighthouse Drawings: Joe Seney
Illustrations: Greg Irons

Editor, Sunset Books: David E. Clark

Front Cover: Beach, Santa Barbara. Back Cover: Russian Gulch, Mendocino County. Title Page: Sonoma County shore. Unless otherwise noted, all photographs are by Jack McDowell.

Third printing September 1981
Copyright © 1975, 1978, Lane Publishing Co., Menlo Park, CA 94025. Second edition. World rights reserved. No part of this publication may be reproduced by any mechanical, photographic, or electronic process, or in the form of a phonographic recording, nor may it be stored in a retrieval system, transmitted, or otherwise copied for public or private use without prior written permission from the publisher. Library of Congress No. 75-58504. ISBN 0-376-05184-1.

This book was printed and bound by Kingsport Press, Inc., Kingsport, Tennessee, from litho film prepared by Balzer-Shopes, San Francisco, and Graphic Arts Center, Portland, Oregon. Body type is Helvetica; type for heads is Helvetica and Americana Black, composed by Haber Typographers, Inc., New York. Paper for the body is Velvo Enamel made by Westvaco, Luke, Maryland.

Weed in setting sun, Palos Verdes

Contents

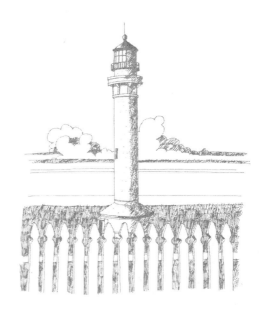

California's

A Thousand-Mile Meeting

California's western edge is alive! Drive for a few miles on the sinuous coast highway, taking in a comprehensive view, or stroll a length of shore, inspecting the endless variations in sea and sand. Every inch is active, pulsating. Changing slowly under the natural processes of the earth or being altered quickly with man's works, the coast is more than a static collection of places. It is a dynamic entity.

For 1,100 miles up and down the state stretches the coast of California, spreading out from the water's edge to encompass offshore islands as well as seaward slopes of the westernmost mountains. The coast is a zone of unique geologic structures, life forms, climates. It is a valuable natural resource, a place for recreation, solitude, study. For those first experiencing California, seeing its coast can be an exhilarating discovery. For those who know the state well, realizing what the coast really is and what it could become is an enlightening *re*discovery.

SHAPING OF THE SHORE

Like California's people, its coast is youthful. Wave-cut terraces that rise in great steps from the shoreline indicate geologically recent

Western Edge

Place of Land and Sea

uplifts in the earth's crust, drops in sea level, or combinations of the two processes. At present the shore appears to be stable or slowly subsiding, as evidenced by cliffs formed by prolonged wave action at the same level.

Because waves come from the ocean, the sea is chief architect of the coast, and when sea meets land, the latter can only react defensively. In one place it folds or faults upward; in another it accumulates sediments to extend itself. But always the forces of waves, wind, and rain cause the land to give way.

The Pacific is the most active natural force at work along California's shore. Nevertheless, the substance of the earth determines just how the shore will be shaped. In the north, waves pound at rocky headlands—picking at stony cliffs to dig deep caverns and coves, sculpting arches that collapse to leave bold sea stacks. Chunks of land are pulverized and deposited in coastal indentations where they form pocket beaches as the sea endeavors to straighten the sawtooth shore.

Below Point Conception, though, the east-swinging coastline undergoes dramatic changes. Here, sand-laden currents flow along the shoreline, smoothing it and laying down an almost unbroken curve of wide beach. Cliffs are still present, but they stand back from the water. It's as if they were tamed in spirit as well as in form by the sea that gnaws them, the civilization that crowds them.

Thistle heads, Palos Verdes

THE NATURAL WORLD

Just as the sea physically changes the shore, so does it create numerous other coastal conditions collectively known as "environment." Tending to cool much of the north, the powerful California current neglects to turn Point Conception's corner. As a result, warmer waters in the south radiate their influence landward. Here, temperate-climate species of plants and animals approach the southern limits of their range, mixing with semitropical species reaching their northern boundaries.

Differences are apparent all along the coast. To the far north, winter rains and summer fogs nourish redwoods, firs, and spruce, and a system of streams and rivers flourishes. Around the Golden Gate, signs of dryness appear. Chaparral covers many slopes; rivers become fewer, finally giving way to seasonal streams. Breathtaking as its landscape is, California's coast possesses even more valuable natural resources: forests in the north, oil in the south, and a wealth of wildlife in between. Estuaries and wetlands teem with migratory fowl, shore birds, spawning fish, and organisms essential to the natural food chain. Offshore kelp beds harbor entire colonies of marine life. Otters, seals, and sea lions gambol in the surf. Rocky pools form a natural aquarium for small creatures dependent on the rise and fall of the tides.

BOB EVANS
Sea lions, San Miguel Island

Fish in kelp, Monterey

8

Gulls, Long Beach

Feeding pelicans, Anacapa Island

THE PRESENCE OF MAN

For hundreds of years man's presence scarcely disturbed this coastal environment. But in the last half-century, greater wealth, more leisure, and sheer population pressures have subjected the California coast to the often destructive influence of civilization. From north to south, the general trend is a shifting from rural (even primitive) regions to increasingly urban ones. Spreading centers of intense development are evidence that many miles of shore have been usurped from nature's proprietorship.

The damage caused by man's presence has not been light, and the list of his transgressions against nature can be recited with what is, by now, a tired familiarity. Sewage outfalls and discharged wastes foul beaches and estuaries. Industrial and agricultural contaminants threaten the ability of shore birds and mammals to reproduce. Oil spills stain the sands and kill unknown numbers of creatures. The sight of oil rigs defiles many beaches and offshore waters.

Deluded by the same false picture of plenty that caused the gray whale to be hunted to the edge of oblivion, man overfishes the coastal waters and strips the tidal lands. He fills and develops thousands of acres of wetlands, seriously shrinking vital wildlife habitats and

9

endangering or eradicating many species. He covers agricultural land with residential and industrial structures. He dams and diverts rivers, cutting off the major sand supply of beaches. He builds obstructions such as break-waters, which further disturb sand transport and cause stripping of the shore. In rural areas many problems are created by mismanagement of resources—land erosion frequently results from improper timber cutting.

Populated areas have their own share of troubles caused by sheer overcrowding: traffic jams, full parking lots, and packed strands are often the summer weekend norm. Blocking what should rightfully be everyone's view are omnipresent highrise buildings. Poorly planned housing sited on unstable bluffs causes earth slumping and property damage. Landowners wishing to protect a bit of shore from misuse—or anxious to preserve their privacy—post "no trespassing" signs and erect fences, denying public access to the shore.

DEFENDING THE COAST

Grievous though it is, man's record is not all bad. Enlightened voices have spoken in the past against reckless exploitation, and such precious resources as Torrey pines, gray whales,

San Diego Bay

Laguna Beach

San Francisco

Mission Bay

Eureka dock

and sea otters have been protected. Parks have been established to preserve important parcels of land. Man is realizing that to tilt the delicate balance in one place is to cause a train of disruption that circles back to directly affect his life. He is learning that the concept of limitless wealth is a false one.

Increasingly, conservation-minded individuals and groups have rallied to the coast's defense. In late 1975 the California Coastal Zone Conservation Commission—created in 1972 by statewide referendum—offered to the legislature a master plan for coastal use. The plan's stated aims were to preserve the coast for the benefit of present and future generations and to allow it to meet human needs in a manner that safeguards its natural integrity.

The issues raised are thorny. For example, public access to the shore is accepted as of primary importance. But how can this principal be judiciously applied to allow everyone to use the shore without denying the individual the experience of solitude? What about the rights of land owners over whose private property the public must pass in order to reach the coastal strip? And how can the needs of civilization be accommodated so as not to conflict with the processes of nature?

It's more than a scenic world of waves and sunsets, this California coast. It is a living world in constant transition, a vital resource that demands to be respected and deserves to be discovered.

The North

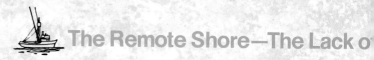

The Remote Shore—The Lack o'

There's no sharp demarcation line, no sign pointing seaward. But in the north, California's long coast begins properly at the Oregon border. Just below the quarantine station, spray blown inland from Pelican Beach whips across U.S. 101, the well-traveled roadway linking those few lonely settlements spotted along this remote shore.

Farthest north of California's coastal towns, Smith River is a pastoral focus of dairying and flower growing. From the foothills to the sea, fields are given over to slim Easter lilies or fat cattle. Smith River sits a couple of miles inland from Pelican Bay, but Crescent City—to the south—overlooks the Pacific Ocean, and this town's island-dotted inshore waters evoke memories of a Japanese painting.

Below Crescent City the highway swings eastward, slipping in and out of Redwood National Park's majestic groves, twisting past Klamath (self-styled salmon capital of the world), and sweeping through Orick, southern terminus of Redwood Park. Though sometimes losing sight of the sea, the road is never far from water in this river-and-stream country.

Beyond Big Lagoon and not far below Patrick's Point State Park, the colorful fishing settlement of Trinidad perches high on a coastal bluff reached by a turnoff from the main road. Close by the highway, comes Arcata, followed by hustling, bustling Eureka. Then U.S. 101 leaves the northern shore, bending far inland as if fearful of the scenic but formidable bulge comprising the jagged hills of Mattole River country and the ragged peaks of the King Range.

Coast

People is its Greatest Charm

There is rapture on the lonely
    shore;
There is society, where none intrudes
By the deep sea, and music in its
    roar:
I love not Man the less, but Nature more.

—Lord Byron

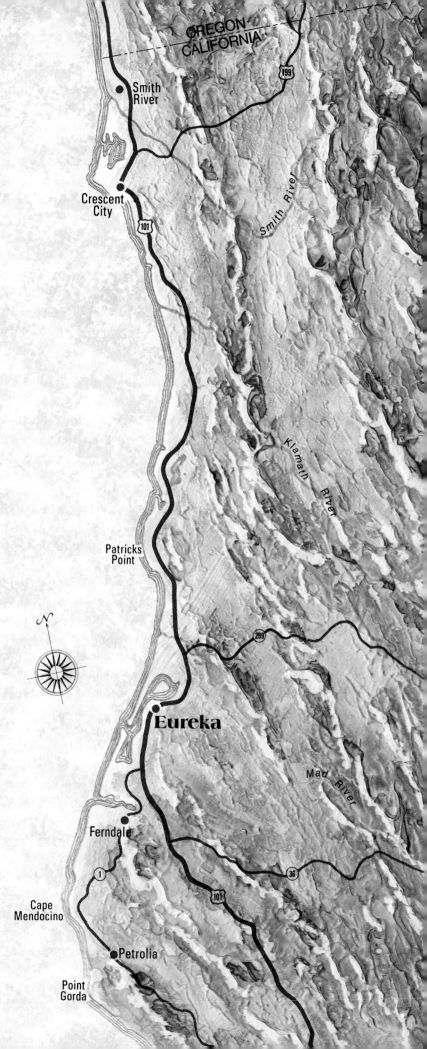

Getting the DRIFT on the unspoiled SHORE

"I like pieces of wood that look like animals," declared the lady from Sacramento, whose high-heeled shoes were fastened to her feet with rubber bands so they wouldn't come off in the sand. "I take them home and set them out in the yard for decoration."

"I'm on pension," said the old gentleman, pausing in his brisk hike along Crescent City's shoreline. "Every morning I walk the beaches and pick up stuff to sell to shops in town."

Seaside visitors are intrigued by finds of flotsam cast up by the ocean. Happily they fill auto trunks with branches and gnarled roots that have been carried downriver from inland forests. Seaside residents are used to having such wrack deposited almost at their doorstep but are no less enthralled by the forms sculpted by wave and weather.

After the kind of November storm that drags drift from one beach to another, shells, gemstones, and mysterious bits of bone strew the sand—all treasures for the earnest beachcomber. Glass floats—some as large as basketballs—sometimes turn up. A lucky find is a drifter, a disc of yellow plastic put into the sea by the Coast and Geodetic Survey to track currents.

NO PROBLEM OF SCARCITY
Knowledgeable beachcombers canvass coves and scrutinize inlets daily, since wave action and tidal movements rearrange such mountains of drift, bringing to light ever-new treasures in wood.

KNOWING WHAT TO LOOK FOR
Worn smooth by friction of sand and wash of waves, glistening beach pebbles attract rockhounds from afar. Jade, opal, and agate are occasionally turned up, as are deceptive bits of colored glass. It takes a practiced eye to spot gemstones in a handful of gravel.

**EASTER LILIES,
AND A LOW-TIDE MUSEUM**
*Cool, moist climate of Smith River—
California's northernmost coastal community
—is ideal for lily culture, below. More than five
million bulbs are shipped annually to
markets throughout United States and
Canada. Weather sometimes isolates
Crescent City's Battery Point lighthouse,
above— a historical museum. Though just
200 yards from shore, it can be reached only
at low tide by walking across the reef.*

We don't have a lot of TOWNS... we've got just ENOUGH

Few in number and populated by independent, individualistic people are the north coast towns. Smith River: "Easter Lily Capital of the World," in the heart of dairy country. Crescent City: Seat of Del Norte County, home of Redwood National Park Headquarters (whose offices are built on tall pilings against a possible repetition of the disastrous tidal wave of 1964). Requa and Klamath: On the banks of Klamath River, famed for its salmon and steelhead runs. Trinidad: Commercial and sport fishing center of the north. Arcata: Home of Humboldt State College. Eureka: Seat of Humboldt County, lumber and shipping center since 1850.

In the words of a lifelong north coaster: "These are good places to live. We don't have many towns up here ... we've got just enough."

OLDEST TOWN ON THE NORTH COAST
Settled as a port in 1850 and incorporated two years later, Trinidad served as a whaling station, later as a lumber shipping point. Today the big interest is in fishing, and commercial as well as private craft crowd the picturesque harbor.

SUNDAY SOCIALIZING
Friends come calling on a lazy afternoon at Blue Lake, northeast of Arcata in the heart of the coast's logging country.

SUMMER SUN, SUMMER FUN
Rodeo at Orick, above, salmon barbecue at Arcata, below, mark high spots in circle of the north country seasons. Other annual events in Del Norte and Humboldt Counties include All Indian Basketball Competition, Old Timer's Day, Crab Races, Rabbit Show, Horseshoe Pitching Meet, and, of course, the county fairs.

"Come on up, the FISHING'S fine"

There's no thrill like that of hooking a rod-bending, record-breaking salmon or netting a wildly wriggling trout. Because some of the state's finest fishing streams empty into the Pacific, their waters—and the inshore waters of the ocean—are happy hunting grounds for anglers of all persuasions. Seasonally teeming with salmon, trout, rockfish, and surf fish, the rivers, bays, lagoons, and deep sea make the north coast a place where all the fishing action is.

The people of the north coast are unselfish about their bounty. "Come on up," they say. "The fishing's fine."

HOIST HIM HIGH!
When salmon are really running, fishermen work the river mouths elbow to elbow. On occasion, tempers flare and someone may be hit with a wild oar, but usually there are enough fish for everyone.

*KEEP AN EYE
ON THE OCEAN
Under an in-rolling wave goes the dip net.
When lifted, it may contain ten or
fifteen pounds of silvery smelt. The wise
smelt dipper watches the surf line, ever alert
for the big wave that might dump him.*

*WHEN THE FISHING'S FINE
Some of the best angling in
California is found along the
north coast. Though
the hottest time for catching
fish depends on a host of
variables, the chart
at left indicates best
seasons for hooking the
more popular species.*

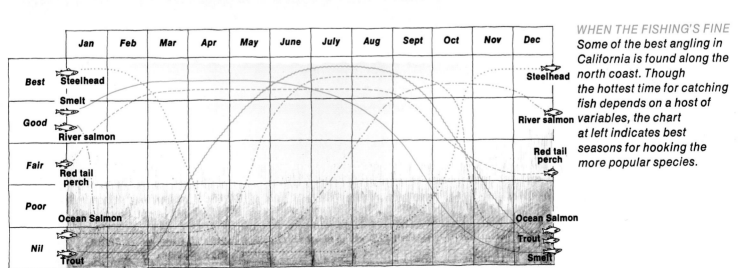

	Jan	Feb	Mar	Apr	May	June	July	Aug	Sept	Oct	Nov	Dec
Best	Steelhead											Steelhead
	Smelt											
Good												River salmon
	River salmon											
Fair	Red tail perch											Red tail perch
Poor												
	Ocean Salmon											Ocean Salmon
Nil												Trout
	Trout											Smelt

**Clams are best taken during low
spring tides; crabs are best
taken December to June.**

**Be sure to consult your Fish and
Game regulations regarding
licenses, seasons, limits.**

21

DOWN IT COMES!
Chips fly as a chain saw chews through a fir, and the faller makes ready to leap clear in the event the tree kicks back as it drops. Skill and potential hazard make fallers highest paid men in woods.

UP IT GOES!
Mammoth claw-front loader is overbalanced by mammoth redwood log. By skill and sheer mechanical power, the operator will maneuver the log closer to his machine and over their common center of gravity, then lift it high for loading onto a flatbed truck.

The
TRACK
of the cat, from
FALLER
to sawyer

The gold rush started it. Though some coastal logging began in the late 1700s, the big boom came 50 years later when it looked as if San Francisco were here to stay.

Historically, timber has been harvested by two basic methods. Selective cutting is a thinning-out process in which larger trees are removed and smaller ones left for future growth. Clearcutting—harvesting all timber in an area—is done when an entire stand of trees is mature or declining.

Downed trees are sawed—or bucked—into manageable lengths, which are then skidded through the woods by "cat" for loading onto flatbed trucks.

At the mill, friction drums, air hammers, pronged blades, or high-pressure water jets strip bark from the trunks. The naked-looking logs move to the headrig, where a screaming band saw slices them into thick sections called cants. Hustled along to ganged circular saws, then to edging and trimming machines, cants are cut tidily into boards. On a moving belt—the "green chain"—boards are graded according to the quality of wood, then go to the air yard for drying.

*WETTING
AND WAITING
Logs stored in a "cold deck" must be kept
moist to prevent fast drying out and
subsequent splitting and checking. Decked
timber is milled in January, February,
and March, when rainy weather curtails
operations in the woods.*

ANOTHER DAY, ANOTHER WAY

Six span of oxen drag a string of logs over a highway made by laying tree trunks crossways. Such a track was called a skid road, a term that evolved into "skid row," meaning an area frequented by alcoholics. Early-day lumberjacks were hard drinkers.

Gunning the Tree. Balanced on a plank staging, head chopper used a gun stick (a scissors-like arrangement of jointed poles) to sight a line where he wanted tree to fall and thus to determine undercut.

Making the Undercut. Working opposite each other on side toward which tree was to fall, two choppers alternately swung away with their long-handled, double-bitted axes to make a deep undercut.

EARNING A DAY'S PAY
Woods crew takes a breather while posing solemnly for the camera. With only sharp axes, muscle power, and skill, men barked, split, and hewed logs into finished planks near the spot where the trees were felled.

Making the Backcut. With the undercut complete and the big block knocked out of the way, two men began to haul back and forth on a long saw, making the backcut on side opposite the undercut.

Dropping the Tree. As saw bit deep into tree, steel wedges were driven in behind it to relieve pressure and nudge tree into the line of fall. A successful fall dropped a tree without shattering it.

*FALLING A TREE
WAS NOT JUST HIT OR MISS*
Around the turn of the century, larger trees were cut than are harvested now (there aren't as many big ones left), and a real giant took three or four days to drop. The trick was to have a tree land on a falling bed made from branches to keep the wood from being damaged.

Redwood National Park: Forests that Existed before Man

SILENCE IS GOLDEN—AND GREEN
For most of the day, sun is filtered by a dense canopy of high growth, and the forest is bathed in deep shade. In early morning and later afternoon, golden beams slant between the trunks, glowing briefly on the soft forest floor.

"Where the fog flows, the redwood grows," is an old north coast saying. And where the redwood grows is a timeless world of natural wonder.

Discovered by a Spaniard in 1769 (Don Gaspar de Portola), collected by a Scotsman in 1794 (Archibald Menzies), and named by an Austrian in 1847 (Stephan Endlicher) to honor an American Indian (Sequoya, a Cherokee), the redwood is one of California's most versatile products—and one of its most perpetually controversial subjects. Flourishing on the coast, the redwood has grown in great forests since the earth's Oligocene epoch over 30 million years ago.

Preserving a remnant of that forest—a forest that existed before the human species evolved upon the earth—is the commission of Redwood National Park.

From above Crescent City at the north to below Orick at the south, Redwood National Park is a blend of rugged coastline, deep forest, canyons, and hills. Land close to the shore is under the ocean's influence. For days at a time, thick fogs may blanket beach and bluff; temperatures are cool, rainfall heavy—all conditions to the liking of *Sequoia sempervirens*. At higher inland elevations, where summer days are hot and dry, redwoods thin out, giving way to tan oak, madrone, Douglas fir.

One of the West's greatest scenic and recreation areas, Redwood National Park contains 106,000 acres, 48,000 of which were added in 1978. To a person not well-versed with the plan of the park, its makeup and boundaries can be somewhat confusing, for the whole comprises three state parks (Jedediah Smith, Del Norte Coast, Prairie Creek) connected by a coastal strip that, in some places, is less than half a mile wide.

SHATTERING THE STILLNESS
Of all park activities, the Great Annual Banana Slug Race, held at Prairie Creek campgrounds, is perhaps the most raucous. As spectators and prompters whoop it up, Chief Running Slug inches across the finish line into the winner's circle.

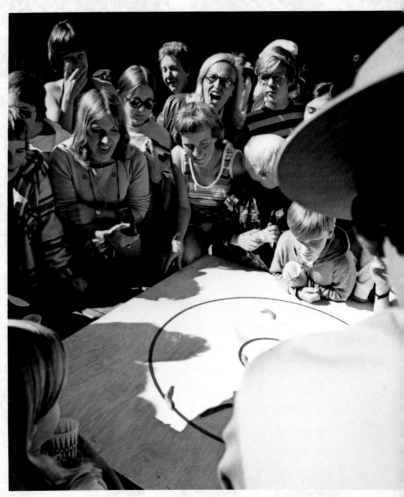

EUREKA is only a gull's flight away from SAMOA

It's the largest deep water port between Portland and San Francisco, and it has two peninsulas bearing the exotic names of Samoa and Manila. Originally settled in the 1800s as a mining town, Eureka quickly grew into a major shipping center. Even when gold petered out in the northern mines, Eureka hardly noticed, because it was already flourishing from a double-barreled boom built around fishing and lumbering. Today these same themes are reflected in many ways around the city at the side of Humboldt Bay, whose waters are churned by fussy boats of the fishing fleet and ocean freighters laden with wood pulp and lumber.

The themes are echoed in the curriculum of California State College—at nearby Arcata—which offers studies in fish and game management, forestry, and oceanography.

BIG APPETITES

Once the Samoa Cookhouse fed work-hungry lumberjacks. Today it continues the tradition by dishing up all-you-can-eat breakfasts, lunches, and dinners for visitors. An accompanying museum features culinary items and tools from the early logging years.

PETER WHITELEY

BIG SHIPS . . . AND
RELICS OF BYGONE DAYS

*Everywhere apparent is Eureka's bond with
the logging industry. At the edge of
Humboldt Bay, stack upon stack of lumber
wait for rail transport across the country
or sea shipment to world ports. An earlier era
of steam-operated donkey engines and
locomotives is recalled at fascinating
Fort Humboldt outdoor logging museum (left).*

MONUMENT TO ORNAMENTATION

Bristling with gables, cupolas, and pillars, the Carson Mansion, located at Second and M Streets, is a breathtaking configuration of incised decorations, massed moldings, and carved eave boards. Constructed in 1885 by William Carson, owner of a profitable logging business, the house was occupied by three generations of his family. In 1950 the mansion was taken over by the Ingomar Club, a group of civic-minded men dedicated to preserving its heritage. The smaller Victorian across the street (right) was built by William Carson as a wedding present for one of his sons.

Clear of the harbor long
before dawn, commercials
make their ocean runs
and are back to unload by
early afternoon. The rest
of the day is spent keeping
gear in order. Long-range
craft—chugging out of
Eureka and Trinidad—pass
weeks at sea, working as
far north as Alaskan waters.

Ferndale—
VICTORIAN VILLAGE at the crossroads of time

As if the name "Ferndale" weren't evocative enough, this pastoral town is also known as "Victorian Village" and "Cream City." Tradition is linked with all three designations.

Ferndale is the original name given to a farm that eventually grew to a community. The appellation is appropriate because of the luxuriant growth of ferns in this part of the fertile Eel River Delta. Since the same rich soil provided ideal grazing for Jersey and Guernsey cows, butter- and cream-making became an important industry. As dairying prospered, many of the farmers built large homes in the Victorian style. Some of the handsome structures remaining on large rural acreages and in town make this one of California's most picturesque settlements.

The houses of Ferndale have a well-scrubbed, well-cared-for look. The elaborately decorated ones—such as the original Seth Louis Shaw home, built in 1853 by the town's founder—resemble wedding cakes. A stroll past the scrollwork storefronts lining Main Street is a trip to another age; stepping into Gepetto's Toy Shop, for example, is like returning to a happy childhood.

Despite its idyllic setting and other-era atmosphere, Ferndale is a place being pulled in several directions and not knowing which way it wants to go. Old-timers want it to be left alone, but they don't want their town to die. They favor refurbishing the old Victorian homes, since this would preserve Ferndale's uniqueness and wouldn't enlarge the town. Yet it is feared that, if refurbishing is carried too far, the result might be a north coast Disneyland kind of place that would invite mass tourist invasion. Then there is the rumored possibility of the state acquiring Ferndale and turning it into a working Victorian village—a sort of Williamsburg West. This makes everyone shudder.

INSIDE
Furnishings of another era grace the interior of many a Ferndale home under the loving care of a nostalgic owner. The television set seems out of place, often giving way to family gatherings around the piano.

*Ferndale greets a new morning as mists
lift from the flat land of the Eel River Delta.
In this pastoral place, one day is pretty much
like another, except for a special week
in May. Then the annual Art Festival brings
creative displays and visitors to Main Street.*

NO GITTIN'. . . JUST SITTIN'
In Ferndale there's no hurry to go anywhere, and not much to do when you get there. The best part of a day can be whiled away sitting on a bench, greeting any neighbors who might happen along.

"Gingerbread Mansion"

"Picket Fence House"

"Gumdrop House"

SMALL TOWN . . . BIG HOUSES
*Back in those days when families were big
and stayed in one place for a long time, folks
built good-sized homes and lived in
them for several generations. In Ferndale is
preserved some of the country's most
beautiful old-time architecture.*

Roaming the
KING RANGE—
California's lost coast

It's one of the state's last pockets of coastal wilderness. It's a ragged, rugged territory of timbered mountains thrusting up 4,000 feet from the Pacific shore, and long stretches of smooth, clean, barely accessible beaches. Some call it the "lost coast"; others call it a wilderness The Bureau of Land Management—which administers its 540,000 acres—designates it a National Conservation Area, the first of its kind in the United States. It's the King Range and it's near Cape Mendocino, some 230 miles north of San Francisco.

The whole place is a kind of pilot model, a multiple-use testing ground for determining if conservation aims, recreational needs, and commercial interests can coexist. According to the BLM, the management program ". . . provides for a balance of use and protection that will enable the King Range to contribute toward the material needs of the nation while preserving the unique seashore environment." In other words, part of the area is to be kept in its wild state, part is to be used for recreation, and part is to be selectively logged, with revenues being used to expand and consolidate the land holdings.

Though the King Range is not a designated wilderness, no roads mar its natural landscape. The only way to drive there is by taking the Shelter Cove Road from Redway on U.S. 101 to King Range County Road. Situated off the rough county road are developed campgrounds (water, tables, toilets). Primitive forest camps are located along trails heading down the west slope.

EVERY STEP
A NEW SCENE
Heavily timbered slopes, tangled brushlands, grassy meadows, rocky bluffs, and isolated beaches offer striking variety for the backpacker. Improved campgrounds, with toilets, piped water, are located off King Range County Road on east slope of range.

VIEW FROM THE TOP
One of the least accessible stretches of California coastline, the King Range plunges from a maximum elevation of 4,086 feet to sea level, in some areas almost straight down.

Mendocino

 The Quiet Coast—Its Slumbering

Tranquil and calm is the greater part of the Mendocino-Sonoma coast, as peaceful as the mists that creep over its capes and slip into its coves. To the north the shoreline is indented with sheltered beaches and punctuated by ragged headlands; southward, the face of the land changes to wooded slopes and grassy terraces that drop abruptly to a sea-chewed shore. Quiet though it is, this coastal region receives a goodly number of visitors because of its proximity to San Francisco.

From sleepy Rockport town all the way south to the Russian River—and beyond—State 1 courses like another kind of river, keeping so close to the shore that it hardly disrupts nature's contours. Slipping across steep hillsides and sliding through stands of cypress and eucalyptus, this stream of a highway flows over countryside that has been trodden by Indians, explored by Spaniards, settled by Russians, and emigrated to by New Englanders.

Here is open country, as honest as the people who live on it. Relatively light is the press of population; yet some parts of the region are feeling the pressure of incipient urbanization. Though decrying "the ills of civilization," some residents of the region desire a degree of economic growth. And despite increasing urbanizing influences that manifest themselves in the form of proliferating clusters of hillside homes, they feel there is enough land, enough open space, to accommodate others without their beloved Mendocino country being devoured by overdevelopment.

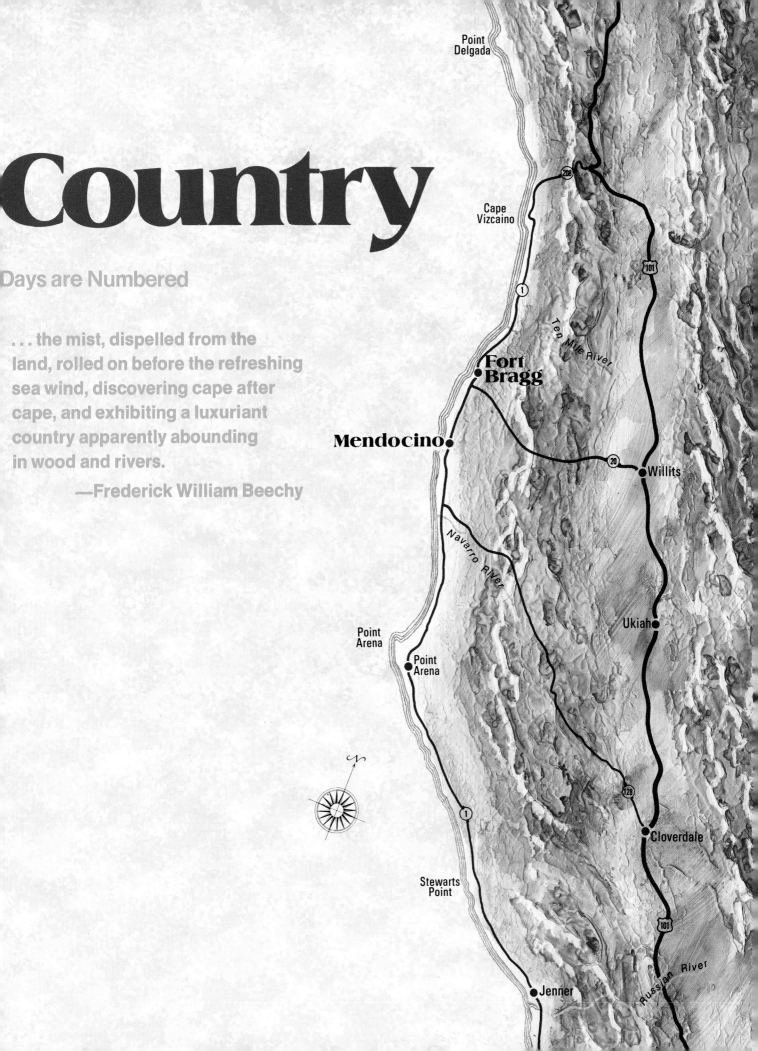

Country

Days are Numbered

. . . the mist, dispelled from the
land, rolled on before the refreshing
sea wind, discovering cape after
cape, and exhibiting a luxuriant
country apparently abounding
in wood and rivers.

—Frederick William Beechy

THE WAY WEST... AND EAST

The direction is due east-west, but for a good part of the trip the track doubles back on itself, aiming the engine toward all points of the compass. At Northspur water stop, steamy sighs of Super Skunk's 2-8-2 Mikado locomotive blend with the happy chatter of passengers who scramble aboard the cab for a glimpse of its workings.

Did you ever ride a SKUNK through the REDWOODS?

Comments weren't complimentary, but sentiment has kept the trains running. "You can smell the dang things before you see them," local people used to say of the first gas engines of California Western Railroad Company, as the locomotives huffed and puffed through the woods.

A logging railroad when it began in 1885, the California Western switched to passenger service in 1904, tugging sleeping cars and coaches on the twisting route between Fort Bragg and Willits. Rolling along as dependably as ever and exhuding more merriment than miasma, the line continues to carry both passengers and light freight along the 40-mile right of way owned by Georgia-Pacific lumber company. Self-powered "Skunk" rail cars run the year around; "Super Skunk" steam trains chug and clank during the summer season.

"GET THEM WHILE THEY'RE HOT!"
The snacks aren't really hot, but Skunk's peanut butcher does a landoffice business dispensing them along with generous amounts of joviality, left. At Fort Bragg an imperturbable conductor gathers tickets from eager passengers.

As you cross over the Noyo River just south of Fort Bragg, you catch a glimpse to your landward side of what looks to be the model for a Norman Rockwell painting of a Maine fishing village. Take the road at the bridge's north end. It drops down to Noyo Flat, a colorful collection of fish processing plants, bait shops, restaurants, charter boats, and commercial fishing vessels. Stroll along the docks and observe catches of deep-water fish being winched out of holds (the commercials leave at 4 A.M. and return about twelve hours later). Sign on for a sport fishing excursion (they also start early). Watch nets and crab pots being mended. Or just sit on a wooden piling—it doesn't matter whether the sun is shining or whether fog lies on the river—and listen to the wood creakings and gull cryings, letting your senses soak up the spirit of the place.

THE QUIET TIME

Processing plants are silent and docks are practically deserted for most of the day when commercial fishermen are busy at sea. A stay-ashore crew spends the late-afternoon hours repairing crab pots and coiling lines in readiness for the next morning's set.

NOYO is everyone's notion of a fishing VILLAGE

THE CROWDED TIME
When weather outside the breakwater is rough, everyone stays in, and the basin bristles with masts. Too broad to fit a berth, one craft has to moor at far end of dock.

Without its FENCES the place would have a lot less CHARM

Time has treated them gently. Weather has alternately bleached and stained them the color of the soil from which they rise. On their posts grow lumps of moss. On their rails spread blobs of lichen. Lurching crazily, they stagger over the hills, starting nowhere, stopping nowhere, only *being*. Green vines embrace their solidity; golden grasses support their frailty. They lean with the dignity of old age and topple with a sigh of relief.

Cleone, north of Fort Bragg

Stewart's Point, Sonoma County

Greenwood Road, near Elk

Near Bodega, Sonoma County

Fort Ross, north of Jenner

Valley Ford, east of Bodega Bay

Mendocino town

Mendocino: The Silent Shore Saved by the State

Peace and quiet are its chief assets. But as more people go there to enjoy its stillness, the less serene it becomes.

ED COOPER

Mendocino's tranquil mien gives little indication of behind-the-scenes turbulence that bubbles up from time to time. No one strolling the silent streets would imagine that in 1854—shortly after its founder, "Honest" Harry Meiggs, took all the money and ran—the mill settlement grew so fast that it almost became the county seat. Mendocino had hotels, saloons, a grand Masonic Hall, a Chinatown. But after the mill closed down, the place fell asleep and snoozed for a long while —until serious artists found the town to their liking and began settling in.

The happy face of the town attracted not only artists and casual visitors but also folks who made up their minds to have a house there. Property values rocketed, new homes popped up like mushrooms after a rain, and residential developments began to appear. It seemed as if the next step might be high-rise condominiums, street lights, and neon signs.

Then the State of California entered the not-so-peaceful-any-more picture. In 1972 the open headland fronting on Mendocino Bay was acquired by the Department of Parks and Recreation with the intent to preserve its natural appearance. The shore was saved, and today a kind of enforced tranquility prevails.

MEMORIES OF MAINE
Shingled roofs and a boxed-in water tower are heritage of early settlers from New England. The ragged shore reminded them of home.

A WALK IN TIME
Some say that the town is too quaint, too contrived, too busy. But when you roam the short streets on a lonely week day, you know that, even with its ever-increasing popularity, Mendocino is all right and will remain that way.

CHANGE COMES SLOW
IN MENDOCINO

"*The town presents a beautiful picture as it is approached from the south on a midsummer's day, with its white cottages, painted business houses, and modest yet beautiful places of learning . . . all basking in the sunlight, with the quiet bay as foreground and the swelling throbbing bosom of the blue ocean . . . and the evergreen pines and fir trees.*" Mendocino today? Yes. And Mendocino almost a hundred years ago, which was when this description was written.

A BIT OF THE PAST,
INCLUDING
OLD-FASHIONED HOSPITALITY

Scalloped coves, open meadows, and cottages tucked into the landscape are part of the experience at Heritage House, located at Little River. In the past a farm, a shipping point, a smuggling base, and a hideout for gangster "Baby Face" Nelson, the area is now a placid retreat for those yearning to escape the ferment of city life.

The old INNS: creature comforts with a touch of YESTERDAY

George Washington never slept in any of them, but that hardly takes away from their delightfulness. Spotted along a 20-mile stretch of the coast highway from Mendocino south are a handful of country inns, some perching on bluffs overlooking the ocean, others snuggled into the foothills on the land side of the road, a few peeking out of tree-thick coves opening onto the sea.

Several of the fine, old structures date back to the mid-1800s. One was built as an executive mansion for a lumber company; one was a grand, Maine-style mansion; a few began as humble farmhouses. Whatever their origin may be, their cozy fireplaces, comfortable rooms, and fine food create a warm atmosphere that cannot be readily found in a regular hotel or motel.

A BIT OF OLD . . . AND NEW
Little River Inn features early California-style rooms with a view of the Pacific. There are also contemporary accommodations, cottage units, and a nine-hole golf course.

OUTSIDE AND INNSIDE
Scrawny wooden gull maintains vigil outside his namesake in Mendocino town. At right, cozy quarters in a cozy hostel.

"It was two days to San Francisco by stage, one by steamer..."

Following in a line of ancestors who came to California from Maine in the 1850s, L.D. Dennen —owner and gracious host of the Heritage House—has been witness to many changes in the Mendocino coast.

"When I was just a kid, it was two days to San Francisco by stage, one by steamer in the winter time. To go anywhere we had to ride four-horse stagecoaches—just like you see in the late, late movies.

"When we went to San Francisco, we first had to ride to Plantation—it's up above Sea Ranch —and there we stayed overnight in the hotel. The next day we'd catch a fresh, four-horse stage into Cazadero or Duncan Mills. There we transferred to the caboose of a lumber train and rode as far as Santa Rosa. From Santa Rosa we took what is now the Northwestern Pacific into Sausalito, then boarded the ferry boat for San Francisco.

"All that took two days. So when people come up to me now and say, 'Goodness, it took us three hours to drive here,' I have to chuckle....

"Weather permitting, we sometimes changed our route by taking the Sea Foam, a little steam schooner that ran along the coast. These schooners got into port only in good weather. When it was foul, they passed us by. But when one made it, we'd get aboard about four in the afternoon, and if there weren't any bad delays, we'd be in San Francisco the next morning. It was a nice alternative. Even though some people didn't take to a sea voyage, it was sometimes the better way....

"I don't remember there being a single stretch of paved road in all of the county when I was very young. My grandfather never was able to go to his monthly meeting in Ukiah as a Mendocino County supervisor without having to ride on horseback, because most of the roads—if you want to call them that—weren't good enough to allow travel any other way....

"There aren't many shipwrecks along this coast any more because of radar and other kinds of sophisticated navigation. Nothing on the scale of when I was a youngster.

"We'd hear the distress signal at night, and everybody in the whole community would jump out of bed and rush to get to wherever the boat might be in trouble to see if they could help.

"My mother used to tell about when she lived in Manchester. There are long miles of beach there at Manchester, which is now a state park. The people would go out and build great fires when a ship ran aground. The ship would be pounding and smashing in the dark and the heavy seas, and some of the men would jump overboard and try to swim toward the light of the fire. Some made it, but many didn't. The loss of life was fearful....

"However rugged this area may seem, the people around here were—and are—pretty civilized. Oh, plenty of tough ones came here, but the rougher elements all ended up in the Mother Lode. The ones that stayed around the coast weren't looking for adventure, like some of the others. They were looking for a new frontier—a place where they could settle down and have a new kind of life and raise a family and work hard for their homes."

AT THE MOUTH AND A LITTLE WAY BACK

Surf rolls and tumbles in constant agitation where it meets outflow of Russian River at Jenner. Four miles inland, wildflower brilliance almost overpowers the mellowed barn-red color of Duncan Mills store-and-post office.

Side ROAD
up the rolling
Russian RIVER

Extending for hundreds of yards into the Pacific below Jenner is a turbulent, sometimes silt-brown expanse of water that marks the end (or beginning, depending on how one looks at things) of the Russian River.

Running low and clear during the summer, the river flows faster—and higher—when winter rains swell it. The river bank road (State 116) twists and turns with almost every bend of the water course, passing through quiet redwood groves and often-raucous resort areas. Hordes of summer visitors know the 12-mile cluster of watering places centered on Guerneville, and many fishermen are familiar with the river's riffles, ponds, and holes.

"REACH FOR THE SKY AND KEEP 'EM HIGH"
Pint-sized showdown on porch of general store is Villa Grande's measure of excitement for the week. (Gas pump prices are a carryover from a more carefree day.) The tiny settlement, north of Monte Rio off Moscow Road, is half-hidden by trees. River road, shown on map above, is sometimes inundated by winter flooding.

Golden Gate

Above and below San Francisco Bay, the timeless sea cuts into soft coastal rocks, sculpting a shoreline of sandy beaches interspersed with low cliffs. Knifing north from the Golden Gate, that great crack in the earth known as the San Andreas Fault has opened a long, sunken valley near the northern boundary of Marin County—Tomales Bay. On the bay's east side, the land slopes gradually, making fine grazing grounds for sheep and cattle whose time is devoted to cropping the sweet hillside grasses. On the opposite shore, the land is rocky, irregular, and dotted with cottages.

Other geologic processes have built high bluffs and ridges overlooking the broad break in the coast known as the Golden Gate. For generations man has armed them to guard San Francisco Bay from other-than-natural forces. One of the few advantages of the perfection of the intercontinental missile was the elimination of a need to maintain a fortified coastline, and the gun embankments and bunkers of the Marin and San Francisco coasts have now become the nucleus of a large, multi-use recreational zone—the Golden Gate National Recreation Area.

In San Francisco—and for several miles southward—the tumbled dunes that once made up the coastline were long ago covered over with homes and highway, leaving but a narrow strip of shore. Much of the once-fertile land approaching Half Moon Bay is yielding to burgeoning development, but below that town agricultural lands are yet prominent.

Coast

Harmony with the Sea

Lo! here we sit mid the sun-down seas
And the white sierras. The swift,
    sweet breeze
Is about us here; and the sky
    so fair
Is bending above in its azaline hue. . . .

—Joaquin Miller

DOWN TO THE BARE BONES

Stove-in hulls almost outnumber sound ones in Bodega Lagoon. At the north end, high and dry alongside Bay Flat Road, there's even an ancient ferry boat. In spite of the protection offered by Bodega Head and by a long, manmade breakwater, winter storms blast across the bay, whipping its waters into a fury, and beating against houses fronting on the water, below.

BODEGA BAY—
beached boats and
mud GRUBBERS

Honoring two towns, a bay, and a headland—all in the southwest corner of Sonoma County—the greatly abbreviated name of Spanish explorer Juan Francisco de la Bodega y Cuadra gives coastside explorers a few moments pause. Just what—and where—is Bodega?

Surrounded by pasture land, Bodega village rests in a valley at the intersection of Salmon Creek and the Bodega highway, 4 miles inland from the bay of the same name. At the bay's north end, a broad peninsula (Bodega Head, once slated to be a nuclear power plant site) hooks out from the shore, protecting the lagoon behind it and the town at the lagoon's edge—the town of Bodega Bay.

Along this shore, the greatest activity centers in and around the lagoon. When the tide is out and mudflats are muddiest, the inner harbor is a favored digging ground for clammers. Commercial fishing boats crowd the town docks, and charters work into the bay and out to sea.

DOWN-TO-EARTH DIGGING
Bay's mud flats attract a strange but dedicated type of hunter: the gaper or horseneck clam digger. When he spots a small hole in the mud or a squirt of water (a sure sign of mollusk activity), he pushes a tin cylinder into the ooze. If shoveling out the muck doesn't turn up a clam, he throws himself totally into his work, scrabbling deep with bare hands. Three feet is the practical limit of the metal tubes, but "sometimes the critters feel like they're thirty feet down."

Leaning barns that once were spick-and-span but whose only traces of care are faded tracks of red paint . . . broken-down harrows, hay forks, and tractors that clattered through the fields but whose silent sides are rusting to the color of coffee . . . sagging chicken coops and pig houses that housed battalions of cackling, grunting creatures but whose only sound is the keening of the wind between the wall boards . . . picket fences that stood tall and tight but whose gaps look like toothless smiles . . . one-lane roads that knew the clip-clop of horses' hooves and the crunch of carriage wheels but whose track disappears into the deep shade of weeds.

MELLOW MEMENTOS
Altered by the alchemy of salt air and time, well-used pieces of agricultural equipment slowly return to the earth.

Touches of
YESTERDAY
in the coastal
QUIET COUNTRY

RICHARD GROSS

PERIOD OF
PASTORAL MAGIC
Late afternoon sun warms the woolly backs of sheep browsing a closely cropped hillside. Haze softens the shoreline, transforming a cluster of rocky islets into ghostly forms.

**SCREENWORK
AGAINST THE SKY**
*Like a crackle glaze on
pottery, winter-stripped
alder branches etch a
webbing against sky and
bay, framing a weary
boathouse whose wharf
ends like a gasp.*

The venerable BOATHOUSES
of Tomales Bay

Tomales Bay once was a handy shelter for schooners serving the farms and dairy ranches out on Point Reyes. In the late 1800s, acres of bay front were subdivided, and the place was ballyhooed as an idyllic resort area, a sailboater's radiant shore. Weekenders from San Francisco used to row on the bay or cruise its waters in launches. During prohibition, rumrunners plied its waters by night, making good use of any available wharf, dock, or boathouse.

Things have quieted considerably around Tomales Bay, and its boathouses are about the only remnants of the "good" old days. Some are sorry heaps of soggy planks while others waver tenuously on worm-eaten pilings. A couple have been metamorphosed into cozy homes.

TRACERY ON THE TIDAL FLATS
Bird tracks, dog prints, shellfish siphons, and mysterious craters pattern the jellylike mud under one ancient structure. Concrete pilings support not only wooden underpinnings but barnacles, limpets, and other forms of intertidal life.

...BOATHOUSES

AS PRACTICAL AS IT IS POETIC
A row of resurrected theater chairs (right) handles part of Saturday night overflow from Marshall tavern and restaurant and makes a fine place for watching the sun set. On the other side of Tomales Bay (below), not far from Inverness, a spidery walkway connects with boathouse supported on toothpick legs.

A WALK OVER WATER

When tide is at flood, you can reach a boathouse easily by skiff, but at ebb the most practical way of crossing over the mudflats is to walk above them. Cheerfully painted "Castellammare", left, is a private residence.

Point Reyes:
Primitive Beauty Untouched
by the Hand of Man

*It's more than a recreation spot.
This island in time increases man's
understanding of the past and
causes him to think about
his future direction.*

The story of Point Reyes is a tranquil story of nature. The story of Point Reyes is also a tempestuous story of man—of his exploration, his exploitation, his conservation.

Coast Miwok Indians were the first known inhabitants of the quiet peninsula. In wonderment they gazed on the ships of Drake, Cermeno, and Vizcaino. It was Vizcaino who gave a name to the land, calling it Puerto de los Reyes, after the Sacred Day of the Three Kings. When California's Mexican governors handed out great chunks in land grants in the 19th century, thousands of acres of Point Reyes became cattle ranches.

The mid-1950s were the most turbulent, most critical period for the peninsula. Real estate developers began staking out homesites; loggers started tearing into the redwoods; oil exploration raised the ghost of derricks and drilling platforms. Spurred by conservationists, the National Park Service moved into action, working at a feverish pace matched only by that of the bulldozers already slicing into the earth. Public pleas were made, petitions circulated, bills fought through. Finally the storm was over: Point Reyes was saved from development.

In 1966 Point Reyes National Seashore was dedicated. Turning the Sierra Club's "island in time" phrase, Secretary of the Interior Stewart Udall called Point Reyes ". . . an island in the nick of time."

ISLAND IN TIME
*This is the very point of Point Reyes, viewed
from Chimney Rock at the upper end of
Drakes Bay. To the right of this narrow spine
of land is Drake's Beach. Though attached to
the California mainland, the Point Reyes
Peninsula is knifed by the 1906 Rift of the
San Andreas Fault, and many geologists
believe it will eventually become an island.*

67

IS THIS THE FAIRE AND GOODE BAYE?

In 1579 Sir Francis Drake brought his ocean-weary Golden Hinde somewhere into a California anchorage. Early writings referring to a "... faire and goode baye ... white bancks and cliffes ..." lead many historians to believe that what is now called Drake's Bay was where the ship was careened for repairs. For them the clincher came in the 1930s with the discovery of a brass plate bearing Drake's name.

NO SHADOW OF DOUBT
Granite cross at Drake's Bay, erected by Sir Francis Drake Association of California, is unequivocally "In commemoration of the landing of Francis Drake ... on these shores."

HERE'S LOOKING AT YOU
White-faced Hereford and Holstein cattle graze some sections of pasture still owned by long-time tenant ranchers. As the National Park Service acquires such lands, fences and barns are removed, gradually returning the peninsula to its primitive state.

The WEATHERED western EDGE of California

Fog, rain, wind, storm. Most of California's weather comes from the west. Cold air slides down from the Aleutians; warm air blows up from the south Pacific. Both are twisted by the earth's rotation to a westerly direction, and the first part of the state to feel climatic change is its seaward side. The coast never becomes as hot or cold as regions several miles to the east because water heats or cools more slowly than land. This is also the reason why seasonal changes along the coast don't follow a "normal" pattern—why summer in San Francisco lags behind summer in Sacramento.

ON A GOOD DAY . . .
During months of October, November, December—and between winter storms— California's coast experiences some of its most brilliant weather. Fleecy clouds are not often formed along the shore but build up several miles inland.

ROY MURPHY

...ON A BAD DAY

When the sky blackens and ominous clouds pile up in the west, dirty weather is on the way. The dark haze between water and cloud layer is an area of heavy rain squalls at sea.

WET IN THE WEST, DRY IN THE EAST

In winter months, warm, moist air blows off the Pacific and is deflected up Coast Ranges, losing heat in its climb. Moisture falls as cold rain on westward side of the mountains. By the time air reaches the mountain tops, most of its water has been wrung out, and it slides down the eastern slopes, growing warmer and absorbing water along the way.

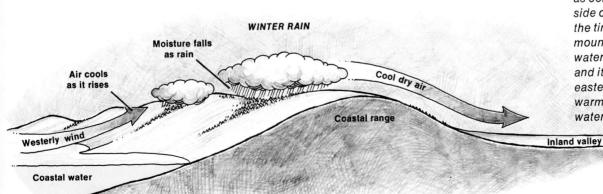

WINTER RAIN

Moisture falls as rain

Air cools as it rises

Cool dry air

Coastal range

Westerly wind

Inland valley

Coastal water

71

SUMMER FOG

Rising hot air

Fog

Coastal range

Warm west wind

Coastal water

Inland valley

CALIFORNIA FOG COMES,
BUT NOT ON LITTLE CAT FEET

Disconcerting to first-time visitors is California's summertime coastal fog. Even inland dwellers, heading for seaside sun, often find their favorite beach completely socked in. There's no out-guessing coastal fog. A few hundred feet in any direction—including straight up—may reveal blue skies.

WEATHER IN A WORD—FOG!
During summer, damp air blows off the ocean toward land. About twenty miles away from the coast, it meets a band of cold water—the California Current—and condenses as fog. Rising hot air inland pulls fog against the Coastal Range. "When it's foggy on the coast," the saying goes, "it's hot in the valley."

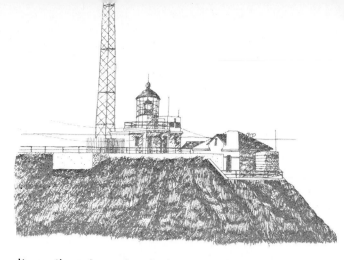

Its northern boundary is the town of Olema, situated at the edge of Point Reyes National Seashore; its southern extremity is Fort Funston, at the foot of San Francisco County. Its 35,000 acres of land and water take in undeveloped coast, state and county parks, military reservations, museums, islands, and privately owned properties that are gradually being acquired for public use. Its setting of rugged, open land, urban park areas, and ocean front makes Golden Gate National Recreation Area unlike any other place in the world.

Much of the Marin headlands at the north end of Golden Gate Bridge was formerly military property. Now the abandoned gun batteries and lonely walls—some of them dating to the Civil War—are open for exploration. Excursions to Alcatraz Island (a maximum security federal penitentiary from 1934 until 1963) and Angel Island (a place of wooded slopes, steep hiking trails, and old army barracks) are adventures in themselves. Among other fortifications that offer an opportunity to relate the history of coastal defense from 1776 are Fort Point, the Presidio, and Fort Mason (headquarters for the recreation area). South of Golden Gate is heavily used urban parkland: Aquatic Park and Pier, Gashouse Cove, Marina Green, Lincoln Park, and Ocean Beach.

The Golden Gate Recreation Area is a place with tremendous use potential. As public awareness of the area increases, more and more people will begin to experience this unique recreational resource.

GOLDEN GATE'S NORTHERN EDGE
Rugged Marin headlands plunge almost straight down to meet waters flowing in and out of San Francisco Bay. Until 1974, most inland area was a vast military reservation, closed to the public.

JUST INSIDE THE GATE
Anglers do their thing at Fort Baker, near the northeast end of Golden Gate Bridge, as a fishing boat chugs along, homeward bound.

Room to RAMBLE–
exploring the Golden Gate
RECREATION area

PETER FRONK

SOMETIMES A SLOWER STEP...
Sunning his back, an old-timer sits for quiet minutes, perhaps remembering busier yesterdays. Since the gradual decline of shipping from many Pacific ports, time has been gentle with some parts of San Francisco's waterfront, harsh with others.

For years Spanish and Portuguese navigators coursed California's offshore waters. But thick fogs and jagged shorelines concealed a narrow gap in the mountain ridges behind which lay one of the greatest landlocked anchorages in the world. Not until 1769 was the magnificent harbor seen by anyone other than native Indians. A land expedition having overshot its objective of Monterey came upon it by chance. Though the group's leader—Gaspar de Portola—was more chagrined than awed, his chronicler, Padre Juan Crespi, wrote of "... an immense arm of the sea ... which penetrated into the land as far as the eye could reach."

Because of the filling of its shallow waters that began during Gold Rush days, the big bay behind the Golden Gate isn't as immense as it once was, but the great harbor encompasses an impressive expanse of more than 400 square miles of water.

Three bays in one, San Francisco Bay is the waterway leading to the smaller San Pablo and Suisun Bays at the north and northeast. Within this maritime region is a waterfront complex made up of more than half a dozen distinct ports (San Francisco, Redwood City, Oakland, Alameda, Richmond, Benicia, Sacramento, Stockton) that handle products as exotic and varied as their worldwide markets. Cargos vary literally from soup to nuts, including wines and wood chips, aircraft parts and almonds.

SOMETIMES A MULTI-LEVEL VIGOR
A truck speeds north over the Golden Gate, a tanker steams west, and a gull matches speed and direction with an inbound sailboat.

DICK ROWAN

SEASIDE SPROUT ROUTE
Rolling past fields of broccoli, artichokes, and Brussels sprouts—and frequently providing easy access to such recreation areas as Pomponio Beach (top)—Cabrillo Highway stretches length of San Mateo coast. However, much agricultural acreage is being elbowed aside by creeping construction.

From ART to ARTICHOKES
along the San Mateo shore

Most of the San Mateo County coastline is open, unbuilt-upon country, and the greater part of the shore is publicly accessible. South of San Francisco, State 1 hurries through several clusters of creeping subdivisions (the ones that inspired the hit tune "Little Boxes"), cuts across some sheer cliffs (that in wet years occasionally let go, road and all), and then settles down to skirting a chain of fine beaches. Along the way are but a few towns —Pacifica, Montara, El Granada, Half Moon Bay—most of them actively engaged in fishing or with a fishing past. Galleries and seaside restaurants attract weekend visitors to some of the settlements, but a large part of coastside San Mateo is not recreation oriented, being given over to such fog-loving crops as artichokes, Brussels sprouts, or broccoli—and to dairy farms. As one eye-catching sign along the highway states: "Our cows are out standing in their field."

HITTING THE BEACH
THE HARD WAY
Winter winds battering the San Mateo coast often tear small boats from their moorings and hurl them ashore. At Princeton, hapless owners trench beneath a beached hull so they can work canvas slings around it to ease the boat out of danger.

HARVEST
IN THE HOLLOW

At Halloween, jumbles of pumpkins attract people from all over the San Francisco Peninsula to Half Moon Bay area. Candidates for jack-o'-lanterns make fall the most colorful time of the year.

HULLS ON THE HILL
Wild grasses hide boat cradles and supporting props at El Granada, making vessels appear to be adrift on dry land, left. Farther down the shore, the glint of autumn sun silhouettes seed heads and shore flowers at Arroyo Frijole (Bean Hollow) Beach.

OUTSKIRTS OF TOWN
On a Spanish map dated April 16, 1839, Arroyo de San Gregorio is shown as part of San Gregorio land grant. In the late 1800s the village was a coastside resort, popular with sportsmen who jounced over the stage road from San Mateo.

Their names are old world. Their look is old time. Their language is Portuguese—with English thrown in for the benefit of outsiders. Lying close to the coast, roughly 15 miles south of Half Moon Bay, San Gregorio and Pescadero are connected by a lovely portion of stage road that ambles over hill and down dale, more or less paralleling State 1.

Once a proverbial "popular resort," the town of San Gregorio (population 150) is today mainly a supply center for surrounding cattle and sheep ranches. Pescadero, with a population of about 1,000, is a more proper-appearing town, with tidy, New England-looking houses, a general store, a restaurant, a tavern, and several churches. A short distance from downtown is a strawflower factory, where locally grown *Helichrysum* are packed for shipment after being wired into bright bunches by women working in their own homes.

In these two gentle communities there is no such thing as a rush hour because there are no traffic lights and few cars . . . and no one is in a hurry to get anywhere.

LIVELY FETE
With music, a parade, a livestock auction, and a barbecue, Pescadero is most active in May, during Chamarita—the Holy Ghost and Pentecost Festival. Spirited bidding takes place in front of I.D.E.S. Hall (initials stand for Portuguese words meaning Society for the Divine Holy Spirit), proceeds going to the local Catholic church.

SAFETY IN THE SEA
*As in a stand of shoreside
trees, the fronds and
stems of* Macrocystis, *giant
bladder kelp, stretch up
toward the sun. Growing
as much as a foot a day
to lengths of over 100 feet,
forests of the great brown
algae provide shelter for
tremendous varieties
of aquatic life.*

BOB EVANS

KELP–
spinach of
the sea

A familiar sight to California beachcombers are the matted tangles of greenish brown "seaweed" that lie strewn about the shore. Contrary to their common name, seaweeds are not weeds but algae—and they are very useful plants. Of the thousands of varieties of seaweed, about a dozen are used commercially. In Asia and Europe, certain types are eaten by humans as well as farm animals. In the United States, "Spinach of the Sea" has yet to be featured on a restaurant menu, but seaweed products are used as a jelling agent in canned meats, ice cream, cheeses, and candy. They are also used for medicinal purposes and in paints, auto polishes, and acoustic tiles. These products are made chiefly from the giant kelp that grows in enormous beds along the California coast. Because harvesting the kelp canopy has an environmental impact on marine populations that dwell in it, cutting is done under regulation of the California Fish and Game Commission to prevent depletion of this valuable natural resource.

SHELTER IN THE STRANDS
At the surface an otter waves a casual paw while wrapped in kelp to keep from drifting away; at the base a kelpfish peers out of his home in the holdfast (root system); on the ocean floor a spotted nudibranch snails his way through anemones clustered between kelp attachments.

MICK CHURCH

BOB EVANS

BOB EVANS

85

California's earliest coastal navigation lights were probably an oil lamp placed in a cottage window or a lantern hung on an oar jammed into the sand. When lighthouses were first constructed on the west coast in the mid-1850s, their design was based on those long in operation in New England: a white tower rising from a tidy Cape Cod dwelling. The first station, installed in 1854 on Alcatraz Island, was followed by others around San Francisco. (Before construction could begin at the Farallon Islands, the Coast Guard had to send an armed party to reason with men who gathered sea bird eggs there and who were reluctant to let the builders land.)

St. George Reef
•CRESCENT CITY

Trinidad Head

EUREKA

Point Cabrillo   •FORT BRAGG

Point Arena   •POINT ARENA

•BODEGA BAY
Point Reyes   Alcatraz
Farallon
Point Bonita
SAN FRANCISCO
Pigeon Point
•SANTA CRUZ
Point Pinos
•MONTEREY
Point Sur

Piedras Blancas

•MORRO BAY
San Luis Obispo

NORTHERN CALIFORNIA'S CHAIN OF LIGHT
Twelfth Coast Guard District—headquartered in San Francisco—administers stations above Point Arguello, most of them land based. An exception is St. George Reef light, which perches on a sea-washed rock six miles out in the ocean.

A CANDLE-LIKE BEACON
Housed in a reinforced concrete tower, Point Arena light is 115 feet above sea level. This is 35 feet lower than its predecessor, whose tower and lens—lighted in 1890 —were demolished in Northern California's 1906 earthquake. Window drapes are pulled during the day to keep sunlight off the lens.

Letting the
LIGHT shine forth

SOME SQUAT, OTHERS SOAR
Point Bonita light, left, crouches at north side of Golden Gate. In 1855 the station boasted the coast's first fog signal, a cannon that thundered into operation in August. By October the sergeant in charge was ready to desert his post, having—in three days—snatched only two hours's rest. Piedras Blancas light, below, thrusts skyward north of Morro Bay.

A LIGHT . . .
*Stately Pigeon Point light
is a landmark for motorists
driving the coast highway
between San Francisco
and Santa Cruz. Named
after Carrier Pigeon, a ship
that piled up twenty years
before the station was
installed, the light can be
seen eighteen miles away.*

PETER CAPEN

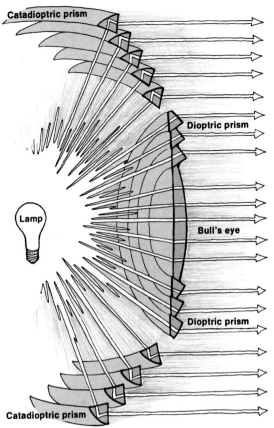

FRAN COLEBERD

... AND A LENS

Ring-shaped dioptric prisms refract light rays and catadioptric prisms reflect them, directing a beam along a single horizontal path. Sets of prisms and bull's eyes are arranged into a series of panels, as in the San Luis Obispo lens, left. When the entire lens revolves around a light source, an observer sees a concentration of rays, or a "flash."

Locals claim that SANTA CRUZ is the SUNNY side of the bay

Except for its elegantly restored and refurbished downtown, Santa Cruz is a little like an old shoe. Worn around the edges, a bit sprung at the seams, somewhat faded—but comfortable and loved. Residents, visitors, and even passersthrough sense a simple air, a down-to-earth hominess that contrasts with the elegance and polish of Monterey. It's an intriguing mixture of tiny summer cottages (most of them ancient), well groomed Victorian homes, and starkly modern structures.

The town has long been a San Francisco Bay Area summer tourist terminus. Locals take pride in pointing out that it's the climate that draws people to Santa Cruz and the adjoining towns of Capitola, Aptos, Rio del Mar. When fog sits over the inland valleys, Santa Cruz is almost sure to be sparkling. And during summer hot spells, San Jose folks head for you-know-where to cool off.

For further diversion (such as Pokerino, Skee Ball, and the Giant Dipper), everyone goes to the lovable old Boardwalk, one of the finest amusement parks left in the country. It's crowded to capacity in the summer. So are seven state parks and beaches spotted along the Santa Cruz shore, all offering a place in the sun.

MAN IS THE MAKER

Before hordes of people settle on Santa Cruz Beach, early-morning bikers savor a quiet moment near Municipal Wharf. Topside are gift shops, restaurants, fish markets. The wharf and an amusement park boardwalk fronting the beach offer diversions for fun seekers.

NATURE IS THE ARCHITECT

Between Point Santa Cruz and Natural Bridges State Beach, the Santa Cruz shore is a haven for solitude seekers. Under constant attack by smashing waves and stiff breezes, the two-mile stretch of sandstone arches and crumbling cliffs is one of the favored places along the Golden Gate Coast to experience the setting sun.

*FISH AND FUN
FOR EVERYONE*
*Once a port for ships loading produce from
Salinas Valley, Moss Landing is no less
busy today with action from fishing boats
and anglers, flower stalls and antique
shops. A huge power plant, looming like a
battleship over the harbor, startles
visitors, but some local citizens
like its sparkling night lighting.*

FLOWERS, fishing fleets, and a flurry of FLEA markets

In their defensible eagerness to push on to the good life in Monterey, motorists traveling along State 1 south from Santa Cruz usually hustle right through a coastal sector that may be less endowed with spectacular scenery than the Monterey Peninsula is, but which is important in many other ways. A cool, moist climate, with little damage from frost, makes the upper coastal corner of Monterey County one of the state's principal agricultural areas. Acres and acres of artichoke plants stud the fields (in Castroville a sign arching over the road proclaims that it's the artichoke capital of the world). And there are fields of strawberries, cauliflower, sugar beets, and lettuce— the crop that gives Salinas Valley the name "America's Salad Bowl."

Twisting inland from Moss Landing is a long, crooked arm of the sea—an estuary. One of the most important and most critical wetland resources in the state, Elkhorn Slough is a rich broth of life forms ranging from green algae to blue herons.

ZOOMING IN LOW
Near Castroville, self-styled artichoke capital of the world, a crop duster lays a swath of insecticide over a prickly field of "chokes."

AL LOWRY

Monterey

Monterey's recreational attractions are sur-passed only by its scenic wonders. Together the two are a magnet drawing thousands of visitors annually to this wondrous peninsula. Here, nature's features are diverse and superb, from the dune country below the Salinas River to the white sand beaches of Asilomar and Carmel, from the stately pines of Del Monte Forest to the weathered cypresses of Point Lobos State Reserve.

Readily accessible is the sea from above Monterey to Point Lobos. Farther south, the shore becomes less easy to reach because of steep cliffs, making the motoring experience the most popular attraction.
Since much of the Big Sur back country is protected as the Ventana Wilderness, many important biological communities flourish there, as well as along the shore. Caring little for boundaries, the California sea otter frolics north of its officially designated refuge well into Monterey Bay. Sea lions, seals, and sea birds breed in this region; kelp beds support fish, shellfish, and other invertebrates.

Below the Big Sur area, the shore curves inland to meet two stream valleys that converge in Morro Bay—one of the coast's largest estuaries. Representing "the shore" for much of San Luis Obispo County—and for communities as far east as Fresno—Pismo Beach and Avila Beach are as famous for sunning as they are for clamming and fishing. Between Pismo and Nipomo Dunes to the south stretches a long, jumbled coastline of sandy beaches and dunes.

South

Haunting Presence of the Ocean

... you can see the breakers leaping
high and white by day; at night the
outline of the shore is traced in
the transparent silver by the moonlight
and the flying foam; and from all
around, even in quiet weather, the
low, distant, thrilling roar of the
Pacific hangs over the coast....

—Robert Louis Stevenson

Where the smooth sweep of the bay merges into the wooded headland, nature has worked with consummate skill. Rocky palisades alternate with sandy beaches. Cypress-covered hillsides converge with the ocean's edge. The climate is benign, the air crystalline. The peninsula's three towns—Monterey, Pacific Grove, and Carmel—have grown considerably since the scenery inspired the setting of Robert Louis Stevenson's *Treasure Island.* But an enlightened development company has preserved many acres of forest and shore in much the same condition as they were when first seen by the Spaniards in 1542.

MOOD AT WEATHER'S WHIM
Thin fog isolates a salmon troller lying motionless in midsummer Monterey harbor. At edge of the autumn ocean, below, waves explode against Lover's Point, and every detail of land and sea snaps into clear focus

MONTEREY HARBOR

LOOK OUT UPON THESE WATERS.

THEIR RECORDED HISTORY BEGAN WHEN JUAN RODRIGUEZ CABRILLO SIGHTED THE "BAY OF PINES" ON NOV. 17, 1542.

SEBASTIAN VISCAINO WAS FIRST TO TOUCH LAND, DEC. 16, 1602. HE CLAIMED IT FOR SPAIN AND NAMED THE HARBOR FOR THE VICEROY OF MEXICO, THE COUNT OF MONTEREY.

JUNE 3, 1770 IS MONTEREY'S BIRTHDAY. ON THAT DAY GASPAR DE PORTOLA, THE SOLDIER, AND PADRE JUNIPERO SERRA, FATHER OF THE CALIFORNIA MISSIONS, JOINED FROM LAND AND SEA TO ESTABLISH THE FIRST SETTLEMENT.

FOR 76 YEARS THIS WAS THE CAPITAL OF SPANISH AND MEXICAN CALIFORNIA. HERE WAS THE ROYAL CHAPEL, THE PRESIDIO AND THE ONLY CUSTOM HOUSE. THEY STILL STAND NEARBY.

IN 1818, BOUCHARD, THE ARGENTINE PRIVATEER, SAILED INTO THE BAY AND SACKED THE TOWN. IN 1842, COMMODORE T. AP CATESBY JONES, U.S. NAVY, UNDER THE MISTAKEN BELIEF THAT WAR HAD BEEN DECLARED AGAINST MEXICO, SEIZED THE PORT BUT WITHDREW AFTER THREE DAYS.

ON JULY 7, 1846, WAR ACTUALLY HAVING BEEN DECLARED, COMMODORE JOHN DRAKE SLOAT, COMMANDING A SQUADRON OF THREE SHIPS, RAISED THE 28 STAR FLAG OF THE UNITED STATES OVER THE CUSTOM HOUSE, TAKING POSSESSION OF A GREAT WESTERN TERRITORY NOW FORMING ALL OR PART OF SEVEN STATES.

THREE YEARS LATER, IN 1849, MANY DELEGATES TO THE STATE'S CONSTITUTIONAL CONVENTION ARRIVED BY SHIP.

ON THESE SANDS IN 1879, WALKED ROBERT LOUIS STEVENSON, DREAMING THE PLOT FOR "TREASURE ISLAND."

FROM 1854 UNTIL THE EARLY 1900'S MONTEREY WAS A WHALING PORT AND THE BEACHES WERE WHITE WITH WHALE-BONE. SAILS CAME TO DOT THE BAY. LATER, IN THE 1930'S, HERE WAS THE GREATEST SARDINE FISHERY IN THE WORLD.

LOOK OUT AGAIN UPON THESE WATERS. MONTEREY HARBOR IS SMALL, BUT IT HAS MADE HISTORY.

HARBOR UNDER THREE FLAGS
Plaque recording Monterey's multicultural history is near entrance to Fisherman's Wharf, town's number one tourist attraction. Wharf's ancient planks and pilings resound to constant footsteps, but casual visitors seldom view its lovably seedy water side.

DICK ROWAN

CULTIVATING THE CASUAL AIR
Elf-forest architecture of Carmel-by-the-Sea
has its detractors, but this tidy settlement
south of Monterey enjoys an offhand
atmosphere that draws year-round visitors
from afar. Sandy crescent of Carmel's
beaches invites sun bathers and strollers
even in winter.

SHORT HOLE, TALL TROUBLE
Seventh hole at Pebble Beach is only 110
yards, but weekend golfers (and sometimes
pros) have sent many a windblown shot into the
surrounding sea. Home of the Crosby Pro-Am
Tournament, Pebble Beach is one of five spectacular courses in scenic Del Monte Forest.

SHERRY GELLNER

SEALS, sea LIONS, and sea OTTERS

GERALD FREDRICK

SEEING EYE TO EYE

Phlegmatic as a banana slug, a male elephant seal stares down an intruder on his domain. The ungainly creature may appear to be stranded, but he hauled his own bulk up on the beach, and, if he chooses to return to the water, he can move with ponderous speed. The numbers on his hip were put on by marine researchers.

A PANEL OF PINNIPEDS

Though seldom found all in the same company, the flipper-footed mammals depicted in the drawing are species most representative of those seen along California coast.

Stellar Sea Lion. Color tawny or yellowish brown; size to 13 feet and 1,800 pounds for males, 9 feet and 600 pounds for females. Seen at Año Nuevo Island, between San Francisco and Monterey; Farallon Islands off San Francisco.

Northern Fur Seal. Males dark brown with gray neck and shoulders, females and young more grayish with light patch across chest; 7-8 feet and to 700 pounds for males, 4-5 feet and 130 pounds for females. Seen at San Miguel Island, off Santa Barbara.

The hoarse bellow of the sea lion is sweet music to people who live along the coast. Commonly seen swimming near shore or hauled out on rocks, seals and sea lions move on land by an ungainly squirming or humping motion. The sea lion, which can rotate its hind flippers, is comparatively graceful on land; this intelligent animal is best known as the performing "seal" you see at amusement parks.

The California sea otter, found in greatest numbers from Monterey Bay south to Morro Bay, spends most of its life in the water. Its favorite food is shellfish—particularly abalone. Surfacing with its prey and a rock, the otter balances them on his belly, then dashes them together to break open the shell.

When Lewis and Clark reached the Pacific, they noted the "sea-orter pole-cats" whose coats were so thick and silky. Their report brought an invasion of American fur hunters, who continued the mass slaughter of otters already occurring off the coasts of Alaska and Canada.

WATER SPORTS
A familiar scene to coast watchers, sea lions cavort near shore, as clownlike in the wild as they appear in animal shows. Scuba divers frequently have freshly speared fish stolen from them by mischievous—and hungry—sea lions.

AL LOWRY

"HEY! WHO ARE YOU?"
Looking every bit a grizzled gentleman, an otter raises his hind flipper and regards the portrait photographer. Intensely curious and nonaggressive, otters will let skindivers approach to within a couple of feet before diving. Unlike other species, the California sea otter spends almost all of its life in water, seldom coming ashore.

Elephant Seal. Males have bulbous snout, are brown or silver-gray; females are same color; 15-16 feet and to 5,000 pounds for males, 11 feet and 1,700 pounds for females. Seen at San Nicolas Island, off Santa Barbara; Año Nuevo Island.

Harbor Seal. Chunky shape, no external ears, squarish muzzle, backward-pointing hind flippers, mottled grayish color; size 5-6 feet and 250-300 pounds for males, slightly smaller for females. Seen in San Francisco Bay; at San Nicolas Island.

California Sea Lion. The trained "seal" of marine shows. Males dark brown, females light brown; 7-8 feet and 500-1,000 pounds for males, 6 feet and 200-600 pounds for females. Seen on Channel Islands off Santa Barbara: at Point Piedras Blancas, northern San Luis Obispo County.

A BEACH
is sand
on the move

Beaches are dynamic creations of winds, waves, and currents. Responding to the slightest change in these shaping forces, a beach face constantly remolds itself, seeking equilibrium. Pockets of beach between cliff and sea that are typical of Northern California indicate a youthful, rising shore; erosion and sediment transport have barely begun. Wave action gradually straightens a shoreline, letting currents deposit continuous stretches of sand, as in Southern California. As more inland dams impound the major supplies of new sand and more breakwaters disturb sand-carrying currents, dredging and hauling must be resorted to in order to maintain what were once natural beaches.

ONE DAY IT'S SAND . . .
Smooth sand beaches are the result of sea cliff erosion and of rivers and streams bringing quartz particles directly to the shore. Though such beaches lose sand to wave action, they are replenished by currents that run parallel to the coast—usually in a north-south direction—carrying sand grains with them.

. . . THE NEXT DAY IT'S ROCKS   *A beach is a fragile and fluid thing. Cobbles pave many shores where storm waves or natural transport have removed sand grains. But rocky beaches can also result from manmade breakwaters or marinas, which reroute the southern drift and—by stopping new sand from coming in to the beach—prevent beach recovery.*

A BEACH IN SUMMER

In summer, gentle wave action lifts grains from the underwater beach face and nudges them shoreward, piling sand into a low terrace called a berm. As typified by Zuma Beach (north of Santa Monica), below, the summer berm is wide, most of it beyond reach of all but the biggest high-tide waves. This is the part of the beach where sun bathers frolic.

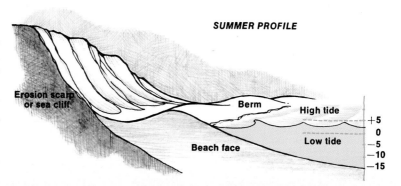

SUMMER PROFILE

Erosion scarp or sea cliff

Berm

High tide

Beach face

Low tide

+5
0
−5
−10
−15

WINTER PROFILE

Erosion scarp
or sea cliff

Berm — High tide — +10
— +5
— 0

Beach face — Bar — Low tide — −5
— −10
Trough — Bar — −15

A BEACH IN WINTER

*In winter, larger waves that strike shore
more closely together nibble away at
the berm, tumbling sand out to deeper
water where it forms bars. In some areas
—such as Oceanside (San Diego County),
above—rough winter surf removes great
amounts of berm sand. Low tide then exposes
heavier rocks that tend to resist shifting.*

Point Lobos: The Greatest Meeting of Land and Water

The many-fingered promontory of Point Lobos has survived the abuses of man almost intact. At various times before the state acquired it in 1933, cattle grazed the meadows, some parts were plowed for farming, and people with an eye for scenic homesites proposed a town on the knolls and ridges. Today, Point Lobos and 750 acres of surrounding sea floor comprise a reserve that is carefully regulated to remain a wild place for wild things.

An extravagant 300 plant species and 250 bird and animal species appear here in their seasons. Sea otters, sea lions, and migrating gray whales are frequently seen offshore; brown pelicans, diving cormorants, loons, and gulls reside on rocky islets. Springtime brings a crazy quilt of buttercups, lupine, poppy, and other wildflowers.

The best of Point Lobos must be explored by foot trail. Along the south shore, low tide exposes a fertile intertidal zone. The north side of the peninsula has ghostly groves of the vanishing Monterey cypress. Paths in the interior lead from open fields into dense stands of tall pines.

THE EVER-CHANGING LAND
Northernmost point in the reserve, guano-frosted Pinnacle Rock takes full impact of wind and wave but dissipates their force only slightly. Interaction between sea and shore is a natural process whose effects are dramatically apparent in this place protected from the not-always-helpful hand of man.

No one tidies the unkempt forest floor or trims the ungainly trees. The only accord is that of nature, a silent harmony into which man must fit himself.

A wild coast and lonely–
BIG SUR COUNTRY

South of Point Lobos, the brooding Santa Lucia Mountains shoulder close to the sea. As if in retaliation, the Pacific throws its weight against the cliffs, creating the mist and thunder that haunt this solitary place. The remoteness of Big Sur has delayed human intrusion. So have its capricious weather and rugged terrain. The few people who inhabit this part of the coast are an independent breed, in turn inspired and overpowered by the Olympian grandeur surrounding them. On one side of State 1 lies roiling ocean; on the other is primordial mountain forest that encompasses the southernmost stands of coast redwoods. Persistent summer fogs sifting into canyons that are gilded by sunsets over an iridescent sea are commonplace, almost surreal occurrences in this uncommon country.

THE BRIDGE AT BIXBY CREEK
Almost hidden by hills and headlands, the graceful center span of Bixby Bridge arches 260 feet over a deep gorge. Twisting and curling for some fifty miles, the coast highway is slow driving but one of the most scenic north-south routes in California.

THE SEA AT
SADDLE ROCK

Only thirteen miles south of Big Sur post office is Julia Pfeiffer Burns State Park. One of its trails overlooks a waterfall that plunges straight down into the ocean. Park was once a grand estate, and many garden walls remain, half-hidden by wild growth.

WHERE ARE ALL THE PEOPLE?

In a fifty-mile stretch of the Big Sur live only about 500 people. Winter washouts and landslides often obliterate portions of the precarious highway, making homes—most of them well concealed anyway—even more inaccessible. Occasional mailboxes along the highway are about the only evidence of habitation.

WHO LIVES
IN THE BIG SUR?
Contrary to legend, there is no "art colony," since working artists who settle here generally keep to themselves, as do ranchers who live back in the hills. Residents and guests of Esalen Institute—a cultural center dedicated to expanding the human potential —roam the coastline, getting close to nature.

WILDLIFE
is the coast's
ENVIRONMENTAL
barometer

Bittern

Field mouse

Green frog

Though examples of wildlife extinction by slaughter are spectacular, only a few of the species listed by the government as rare or endangered have declined at the hand of the hunter. Most are victims of extensive habitat disruption and pollution. As man bulldozes coastal wetlands, meadows, and forests for homesites and industries and discharges his waste into the air and ocean, wildlife diminishes.

Even the most confirmed city dweller depends on food and uncontaminated water from the same lands and waters that harbor most wildlife. A few species— squirrels, gulls, opossums, raccoons—can adapt to man's altered environment, and their presence should not be taken as a sign of a healthy ecological balance. Instead, the increase of stillborn sea lion pups and the fruitless nesting of brown pelicans should serve as harbingers of potential disaster for man.

With the exception of the going-away water snake, which was captured on film by Ray Higgs, all photos below are by Tom Myers.

Water snake

Buck deer

Brown owl

Just a little guest HOUSE... with a CASTLE in the basement

On childhood trips to the 240,000-acre family ranch, William Randolph Hearst became so enamored of the site they used as a campground that, when he inherited the property in 1919, he built a considerably more permanent living quarters on the spot: a $50 million complex from which to govern his newspaper empire. Many of the rooms of the main house and the three guest houses—146 rooms in all—were specifically designed to hold pieces of Hearst's astounding collection of European art and antiques, estimated to be worth at least as much as the buildings themselves. (Rumor has it that there is still a dismantled castle in the basement of the main house.) For over a quarter of a century, construction materials and skilled artisans, as well as treasured objets d'art, arrived by steamer at the dock in the whaling village of San Simeon.

Hearst's acquisitive tendencies didn't stop with newspapers and art treasures. To entertain his many prominent guests, he fenced off 2,000 rolling acres for a private zoo. Then he gathered wild animals from around the world to fill it. Though the zoo was later closed, herds of zebra, elk, and Barbary sheep still roam the nearby hills.

Today the Enchanted Hill—as Hearst called it—is a State Historical Monument. For a few hours, anyone who can afford the entrance fee can experience vicariously the opulence of a life style in which money was no object.

The incredible antiques seem as endless as the tremendous, sweeping vistas of ocean and mountains. The view from the estate itself is of an untamed land. But the visitor parking lot below is often packed with cars and tour buses, and just below San Simeon, wild coast begins to give way to civilization. A clutter of neon signs on establishments catering to the castle crowds hints of the development to be repeated on a grand scale farther south.

THE OWNER'S FAVORITE ROOM
Gleam of antique silver is reflected in polished walnut of Refectory's monastic dining table. The magnificent stone overmantel of fireplace rises all the way to a 400-year-old ceiling, which is a series of elaborate, high-relief carvings.

HIS WORKING LIBRARY
. . . AND A PLACE TO SWIM
Gothic Library, below, was part of Hearst's personal suite where he did much of his work. Interior of Roman Pool room, left, is inlaid with acres of Venetian glass and gold tiles.

A BOON
FOR BOAT WATCHERS
"Fishing around here has dropped way off," some experts state in gloomy tones. But Morro Bay always seems filled with tidy vessels, many from other Western ports. Below are depicted some of the types of working craft that traverse this part of the coast.

Bottom Trawler. Drags a net along ocean floor to catch rock cod, sole, red snapper, halibut, shrimp. A good portion of fish taken off the coast are caught by trawlers.

Salmon Troller. Drags bait or moving lures from long, flexible outriggers to catch ocean salmon, fishing from April through September for this finest of coastal game fishes.

Trawlers, trollers, and a ROCK called MORRO

"Fishing's not what it used to be," said the man at the Chamber of Commerce, the corners of his mouth turning down. "But it's bound to get better," he concluded with smiling optimism.

People at Morro Bay fish for almost everything, and the community promotes its charm as a fishing village. Shoreside anglers cast for perch and flounder from piers, beaches, and rocky coast. Low tide finds clammers scratching in the sand. Oysters thrive here—more than 1,000 acres of them—and Morro Bay celebrates their contribution to the local economy each year with a weekend oyster festival. Visitors can wander through the beds and pluck their own bivalves to take home or sample them on the spot in a ready-made stew.

Many commercial and party fishing boats tie up behind the long, sandy spit that protects the harbor. Their creaking ropes, the screaming gulls, and the summer fog combine to create an atmosphere much like that of a New England seacoast town. Looking seaward toward Morro Rock, the 567-foot dome that stands at the entrance to the bay, the picturesque setting is complete, but looking toward shore, the soaring stacks of a power plant claim the dubious distinction of being almost as high as the rock itself.

QUIET DAY IN THE BAY
Between ocean runs, nets are spread on deck or dock for mending. Their brilliance in the water doesn't seem to spook fish. Nor does fog deter a pier fisherman and his feathered friend.

Gill Netter. Sets out a series of nets on ocean floor, leaves them overnight, then returns the next day to haul in catches of sea bass, halibut, cod, and other bottom dwellers.

Albacore Boat. Scatters pieces of oily fish (called chum) to attract albacore and tuna, which are then caught on lines. Albacore boats make up one of coast's largest fleets.

117

Prehistoric dunes have left their mark everywhere along the coast, but California's shoreline today offers only a few hospitable pockets that combine the right elements for dune formation. The 15 miles of shore between Pismo Beach and Point Sal is one such place. There, the Santa Maria River brings down an abundant supply of sand, and the broad river valley invites the prevailing west wind to blow inland freely, sculpting the sand into waves as it passes.

A dune begins when onshore breezes pick up grains of dry sand from the beach face and carry them landward, where they may lodge against vegetation and form a hill. If nothing stops it, a dune will slowly crawl inland as its sand is blown up the windward slope, over the crest, and down the leeward side. As a hill moves, another forms in its place.

Where vegetation can gain a foothold, dune movement is slowed and often checked. A few hardy plants—such as sedge and ice plant—can withstand the burning salt wind on the seaward side of a dune, sending their anchoring roots deep into the sand. Once pioneer plants have taken hold, others begin growing in the dune's protected lee. These, in turn, attract hungry deer and provide homes for small wildlife.

Still, the stability of the dunes rests on a fragile balance. Vehicles and too many trampling feet can destroy that balance, causing sand accumulated over a thousand years to blow away in a decade.

WRITINGS ON THE SAND
Looking as if made by a pair of purposeful creatures walking arm in arm, tiny tracks stitch across wind-formed sand waves, above. Nearer the shore, sand ripples blend into barrier dune, right, sparsely grown with vegetation because of increasing amounts of salt in the air.

ED COOPER

SAND dune country – the land between two WORLDS

MODERATING NATURE'S FORCES
In dune areas where sand threatens to reclaim its own, man slows the process by planting beach grasses and shrubs. Snow fences and other artificial barriers look impressive but are not too effective in stabilizing shifting sands.

VROOM! VROOM!
Spewing sand and bellowing like a wrathful bull, a high-style vehicle roars up the face of a barrier dune. Guadalupe area, just south of Pismo Beach, is noted for its Saharalike drifts. Countless off-the-road enthusiasts race over the mounds aboard pillow-tired contraptions that only a dune buggy driver could love.

PICKEREL/DANDELET

NOT-SO TRACKLESS WASTE

The restless wind and tireless sea constantly re-form the delicate grains into new patterns, no two ever alike. But nature is not the only pattern maker. Always seeking new recreational areas, humans also leave their tracks and traces on sand dune country.

It's supposed to be the CLAM CAPITAL of the world

At Pismo Beach, you can pay a dollar and dig right in. That's all it costs to hunt the sweet-tasting clam that has brought fame to its namesake town. The circular, thick-shelled mollusks live all along the surf-swept sand beaches of the central coast, but they thrive at Pismo, where the sea floor slopes gradually for a long distance. The town has not been remiss in capitalizing on its good fortune. For 30 years it has scheduled a midwinter clam bash to coincide with minus tides, when the best catches are found on infrequently exposed sections of beach. Scores of dungaree- and sneaker-clad clammers come to turn the sand with spades or special rakes. A resident clammer summed up the feelings of local folk: "Everyone thinks the name is hilarious, but they sure come here when they want clams."

YOU CAN'T GET MUCH CLOSER

Pismo's hardpacked beach is an invitation to drive right down to water's edge for a bit of surf casting. Sand and salt may not be the best treatment for a car, but drivers who stay on damp hardpack—out of reach of waves—aren't likely to become stuck.

CATERING TO THE
BIGGEST DRAWING CARD

The greatest abundance of clams on California's coast is found at Pismo Beach, and shoreside stores, below, provide everything for their capture, including quick haul-out for stranded motorists. At low tides the bivalve bides his time about five inches below the surface, within easy reach of a clam fork. Gauge on handle assures that catch is legal size of 4½ inches at its widest point.

It's not hard to see why the Spanish padres chose the pleasant valley of the Santa Ynez River to establish two missions; the land is fertile and the climate beneficent. La Purisima Concepcion Mission, near Lompoc, prospered under these conditions. Although the mission gradually disintegrated after being secularized in the 1830s, a faithful and complete replica has been built on the foundations of the original. Today, exuberant fields of flowers grow where the mission livestock grazed. Uninterrupted sun from May to September helps produce half of the flower seeds grown in the world.

ALONG THE KING'S HIGHWAY
Spidery conjunction of State 1 and State 246 near Lompoc forms a triangular loop that takes in acres of flower fields and La Purisima Mission, above. In front of main buildings of mission settlement can be seen a segment of original El Camino Real footpath.

Turn off the highway to FLOWER fields and MISSION trails

FLOWERS TO FILL THE EYE
It's late afternoon near Lompoc, and field workers take a final stroll down furrows of ageratum, looking for weeds. Brilliant calendulas, right, are raised for cut flowers, as well as for seed.

California's coast can be a CRUEL coast

As any sailor worth his salt knows, the Pacific isn't always what its name implies. Like any other ocean, it has its share of foul and foggy weather, and mariners unfortunate or unwise enough to be caught out of port when the sea is in a nasty mood had best give a wide berth to California's ragged western edge. Point Reyes claimed the state's first recorded shipwreck; in 1595 a sudden southeaster blew the galleon of Rodriquez Cermeno onto a reef. Since then, California waters have chewed up hundreds of ships. Cape Mendocino, Trinidad Head, Point Joe, Point Arguello, Point Fermin—all have taken their toll. But nowhere have there been more disasters than around the Santa Barbara Channel, where the convergence of two climates and various currents at Point Conception stir up especially fearful seas. At any one time almost anywhere along the California coast, at least a couple of battered hulks lie stranded on bars.

SAD SAGAS OF THE SEA

Schooner Mabel Gray, *above, went aground at Redondo Beach in 1904, losing her deck cargo of lumber, her masts, and her dignity. In 1923, Point Arguello was the scene of one of the U.S. Navy's greatest peacetime disasters. Unknowingly off course, a squadron of destroyers piled up on the rocks, right, losing 7 ships and 22 lives.*

BOOM! . . . AND BUST

Steamship Rosecrans, *taking a smashing broadside from the sea after running aground near Santa Barbara in 1912, top left, was battered, but she survived. Less lucky was the schooner* Venus, *bottom right; despite taut spring lines, she was broken apart by heavy seas off the mouth of Navarro River. Bottom left, a 100-ton sperm whale and* Ohioan *were fortuitously beached together at San Francisco's Lands End in 1937. Neither recovered.*

Coastal Santa

South of secretive Vandenberg Air Force Base and its ocean-oriented Pacific Missile Range, Point Arguello pokes a rocky finger out into the sea. Twenty miles farther along the shore, Point Conception follows suit by jutting sharply westward. These bold landforms mark a kind of magical zone in the California coast, for, political boundaries notwithstanding, the sector between them is a definite dividing line between Northern California and Southern California.

At Point Arguello the shore's westerly thrust diverts cold, south-coursing ocean currents away from the land. Rough seas, high winds, and fogs pushing down from the north are effectively blocked or broken up. Beyond Point Conception, the shore makes an abrupt turn to the east. This different lay of the land allows the earth to absorb more of the sun's rays, and the decided western slope of the coastal Santa Ynez Range acts like a giant mirror, reflecting solar energy southward.

Below the 34th parallel, rocky, hard earth suitable as livestock range changes to rich, fertile soil that supports citrus and avocado culture. Chaparral and pine are replaced by palms and other temperate-climate vegetation. The longer sloping coastal shelf smooths waves, and its shallows tempt surfers and sun bathers. As striking a difference as any is evident in Southern California's coastal architecture. Whitewashed walls, red tile roofs, and black ironwork speak not only of local pride in a Spanish heritage but of a more relaxed, languorous life style.

Barbara

Preserving the Placid Air

In the afternoon they came into a
   land,
In which it seemed always afternoon.
All around the coast the languid
   air did swoon.

          —Alfred, Lord Tennyson

SANTA BARBARA
has a different kind
of life STYLE

To the Spaniards who settled this pocket of California in the late 18th century, it was a new land, a land different from their point of origin. Yet something about the blue skies and the bright waters reminded them of home, and they called their new abode "La Tierra Adorada"—the beloved land. Great ranches surrounded the area, and a gracious cultured life developed that made Santa Barbara the social capital of early California.

As 20th century newcomers discover and old-timers insist, Santa Barbara *is* different. Its setting is out of a storybook: fertile mountains to one side, a chain of scenic islands to the other. The climate is superb—more tropical than farther north, more temperate than farther south. Even the long, narrow coastline defies convention. Instead of running north-south like most of California, it stretches east-west. Reflecting its Mediterranean heritage, the prevailing architecture is white-walled, tile-roofed Spanish Colonial. Flowers and greenery prevail. Even the freeway that skirts the town is tropically landscaped.

Santa Barbara didn't just happen. Long ago its citizens realized that if the place was to remain "La Tierra Adorada," people were going to have to work to keep it that way. Most critical issues—such as comprehensive planning, redevelopment, pollution—are targets of citizen action. Like few other cities, Santa Barbara is a place where people are interested—and involved.

"It's not a matter of fighting city hall, here," said a developer. "It's getting along with civic-minded groups that really do their homework. Our own work is cut out for us, but the place shows it in its life style."

MEDITERRANEAN MOOD
Symbols of southern shore, fan palms stand sentinel-tall along Santa Barbara's shoreline, dividing beach from business district. Protected by the Channel Islands to the south and the Santa Ynez Mountains to the north, the city and its environs are blessed year-round by an equable climate.

ANDALUSIAN AMBIENCE
Tiled corridors and curved staircases of
County Courthouse, above, are but a small
part of this exquisite Spanish-Moorish
"palace." The theme echoes softly in the
flagstone courtyards of El Paseo, left, a
picturesque shopping arcade
evocative of old Spain.

A CITY WITH STYLE

When residents speak of their city's style, they are referring not only to a happy potpourri of Spanish Colonial, Mexican, and Moorish architecture but also to a gracious and comfortable manner of living. Santa Barbara is not the typical "tourist town." First-time visitors remember their stay as a most civilizing experience.

QUEEN OF ALL THE MISSIONS

Unusual blending of Roman ornamentation with simplicity of mission style makes Santa Barbara Mission sparkle like a jewel. Tiered fountain is in patio enclosed by monastery buildings that once housed theological students for Franciscan priesthood.

For a different kind of RIDE get on the right TRACK

A foreign Chief of State visiting California expressed two burning desires. One was to visit Disneyland—which he couldn't, to his great disappointment. The other was to ride the train along the coast—which he did, to his great pleasure. Leaders have changed, but the incomparable rail trip remains a most delightful experience.

The long train glides down the fertile Salinas Valley, between fruit and nut orchards, through fields of artichokes, beans, grain. Skirting oil fields at San Ardo, it passes within sight of Mission San Miguel. At Pismo begins a glorious 113-mile run along the coastline with views of Point Conception and its lighthouse, of ominous missile gantries within Vandenberg Air Force Base, of immense cattle ranches. The landscape changes from jutting rocks and dry hillsides to fields of waving grasses and nodding wildflowers, from long beaches to sparkling ocean.

Though there may be faster modes of traveling, few are quite as satisfying.

"HERE SHE COMES!"
Headlights flashing and bells clanging, Amtrak's train rolls smoothly into Oakland depot in the day's early hours. Throughout the morning it runs the level length of Salinas Valley, then begins a winding climb up Cuesta Grade, plunging through tunnels and doubling back on itself.

"WATCH YOUR STEP!"
Early-afternoon sun drenches San Luis Obispo, left, where a few passengers detrain. A couple of hours later comes the sparkling Santa Barbara shore, with glimpses across the channel of Santa Cruz Island, right. A brief stop at Oxnard, another at Glendale, and, as the sun drops low, the train arrives at Los Angeles Union Station in time for supper.

DRIVING
and dining
detour to
DENMARK

To Santa Maria

Santa Inez

Solvang

To Lompoc

Alisal Road

Gaviota

Goleta

Lake Cachuma

San Marcos Pass

To Santa Barbara

You couldn't call it a shortcut. Driving distance along this former stage route is about the same as it would be if you stayed on the freeway. In fact, the sidetrip could take from a couple of hours to a couple of days or longer. It all depends on how completely you surrender to the visual delights of San Marcos Pass and Santa Ynez Valley and the culinary temptations of Solvang, an Old World town founded by Danish Americans. Equally diverting are the frontier-style village of Santa Inez and time-mellowed Mission Santa Ines, fully restored and in daily use.

Whatever your ultimate destination and no matter how strongly sounds the siren call of the coast, this is an inland excursion not to be hurried.

SLOW WAY TO (OR FROM) SANTA BARBARA
Delightful detour bypasses a coastal corner of U.S. 101. Corrugated hills edging Lake Cachuma, right, are backed by rumpled ridges of San Rafael Range. Opposite: In the shadow of Santa Ynez Mountains, Solvang's spires and rooftops look like a scene from a Danish Christmas card.

The Channel Islands:
A Heritage
of Scenic Splendor

Birds, seals, and sea lions are the chief inhabitants of this unique place. For some species, these islands are the only sanctuary in this part of the world.

ROY MURPHY

Thrusting out of the sea off the Southern California coast are eight craggy chunks of land collectively called the Channel Islands.

Most easily seen from Santa Barbara, privately owned Santa Cruz is largest in the chain. Stands of grasses, oaks, and pines also make it the greenest. Nearby is Santa Rosa Island, also privately owned.

Tiny San Nicolas was the lonely, 20-year abode of a solitary Chumash Indian woman, who was marooned when the rest of the island's population was evacuated by mission priests. Today, San Nicolas, San Miguel, and San Clemente are part of a U.S. Navy target range.

Nearest Los Angeles, Santa Catalina is world famous as a tourist destination (see page 175).

Perhaps it says something about the priorities placed on natural resources that the two *smallest* islands—Anacapa and Santa Barbara—are set aside as a natural monument. Both are characterized by steep cliffs, dry hills, and little vegetation. Yet their austere charm—reminiscent of Scotland's outer Hebrides—makes a sit a calming kind of atavistic experience.

THREE ISLANDS IN ONE
At the eastern end of Santa Barbara Channel is a slender chain of three ragged bits of land, so closely joined as to form one: Anacapa Island (left). The dinosaurian spine of Anacapa's East Island stretches down from a plateau to a land link—uncovered at low tide—with its neighbors. The entire archipelago was once part of the mainland. Thousands of years ago, deformation of the earth's crust and a rise in sea level separated land masses from the continent, leaving a series of mountain tops poking above the ocean.

SEA LIONS
AT SAN MIGUEL

Rookery for vast herds of sea lions,
San Miguel Island is also home for one of the
largest known colonies of elephant seals.
Otters and fur seals visit the island; pelicans,
cormorants, gulls, and foxes are permanent
residents. Portuguese explorer Juan Cabrillo
died here in 1543. Although he is reported
to be buried on San Miguel, his grave has
never been found.

Glowing sky silhouettes a shoulder of Santa Cruz Island and isolates Anacapa on the horizon. Twenty-one miles long and five miles wide, Santa Cruz is largest of the offshore islands. It has protected coves, open meadows, and groves of pine and oak. At various times it has been a Mexican penal colony, a cattle ranch, and a sheep station.

SUNSET AT SMUGGLER'S COVE

BOB EVANS

OIL
is a slippery issue
along the
SOUTHERN
shore

Until recent years, Santa Barbara lived more or less harmoniously with petroleum. Familiar with the thick, black stuff that seeped out of the ground, coastal Indians used it to seal their canoes. English seafarer George Vancouver—visiting the area in the late 1700s—mentioned the channel being covered with a sticky substance. As early as 1896, a well was sunk in the channel at Santa Barbara, and in the 1920s drilling began in the Elwood Field, near Goleta.

In the mid-1960s, exploratory drilling offshore—triggered by state and federal lease sales—created an increased awareness of what could be done to the natural landscape by pollution. Citizens and concerned politicians urged a moderate pace, to give at least enough time for further studies, but drilling went on at an increasing rate.

Then on January 28, 1969, oil became a word heard around the world: a blowout occurred in the channel. Although contained at the drilling platform, millions of gallons of black muck, forced out of fissures on the sea floor, washed ashore.

Though the popular villain, the oil industry was quick to respond, paying heavily in hours and dollars to clean up the mess. Equally quick was the hue and cry raised by Santa Barbarans. Today there exists a standoff between Santa Barbara and those who would drill holes anywhere in the vicinity.

A LONG DRIVE

In the heat of the game, a golfer ignores oil platforms, even though one seems to be a greens' marker. Exploration of potential deposits may necessitate boring holes as much as two miles deep through varied strata, right. Because of coastal slope, offshore sites sometimes require less drilling to reach layers of spongy rock that hold oil, but supporting the ocean-anchored operation calls for more massive rigs.

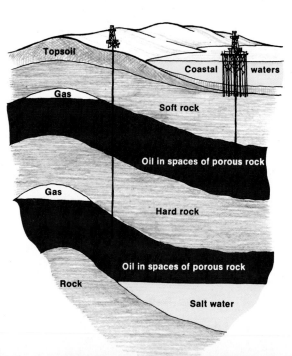

OCEANIC
ISLAND
Looking as if thrust up out of the sea, an offshore drilling
platform looms against the horizon. Supported on a forest of
steel pilings, such platforms are supplied with power and
water from shore, or use self-contained power sources.

The town's real title is San Buenaventura, after the patron saint whose name was bestowed on the last mission founded by Father Junipero Serra. But in 1891 the name of the farming center was abbreviated because it was too long and too difficult to pronounce and because mail was finding its way to San Bernardino.

Though the name is smaller than it once was, the town is not. Ventura, Oxnard, and Port Hueneme—once separated by acres of agricultural land—are now blending into one coastal metropolis. Crowded out by ever-new industry, citrus, celery, tomatoes, strawberries, and avocados are becoming less apparent near the shore.

SAILING
Its canvas holding a breeze, a sloop "stands" out of Ventura Marina, while power cruisers lie snug at their slips. Marina is a casting-off point for voyages to Channel Islands National Monument.

Ventura's
PLEASURES afloat,
TREASURES ashore

SURVIVING
Mission San Buenaventura—built in 1782— has outlived fire, earthquake, Indian unrest, threat of pirate attack, and a craze for modernization. Its museum houses the only wooden bells ever used in a California mission.

SUNNING
Tiny tummies take kindly to salt air and warm sun at State Beach. Despite the presence of numerous commercial developments that seem to lunge out of the sand, the Ventura waterfront is a most enjoyable shoreside recreational area.

A gull skims along a curling wave, its wingtip almost touching the crest, its body motionless, its face impassive. Too sleepy to do more than grumble, a sea lion lazing on a rock watches the bird soar past. Low and unambitious, the surf washes softly over the sand, stretching thin like a wakening cat, before sliding again into the sea. Thin fog creeps back and forth, trying to decide whether to lie over the water or infiltrate farther inland. A pale blob in the haze, a fishing boat slips by, the sound of its engine a muffled chug-chug-chug. When the world closes in on a person, the beach is an open place, a place to be alone.

A SOLITARY SILENCE
Aloneness along the shore brings the feeling that everyone else on earth has vanished, leaving only sky, sea, and self. The ocean-quiet invitation can be to dig, left, or simply to walk to water's edge, right.

TOM TRACY

A BEACH is
a place
to be ALONE

**A SOCIETY
OF SOLITUDE**
*Alone but not lonely, a
stroller and his playful but
silent companion idle
their way down a wave-
washed beach.*

Seaward Los

The Urban Coast—A Will fo

Along the densely populated seaward side of Los Angeles, a few natural wetlands, quiet estuaries, undeveloped mountain tops, and unbuilt-upon hillsides contrast dramatically with the region's urban character. Viewing the coast by land, from sea ,or from air, a traveler is vividly aware of miles of developed waterfront, only occasionally relieved by patches of natural preserves.

Intensified land use along this coastal strip has resulted in a hectic mix of power plants, petroleum refineries, oil wells, and various in- dustrial activities. This is the land of high-rise. This is the coast of condominiums, commercial development, and controlled recreation.

Fronting on upper Santa Monica Bay are several broad strands. Access to these beaches —as well as to the entire coastal stretch from Point Dume to Santa Monica—is provided by the Pacific Coast Highway, a sea-skirting route whose capacity is exceeded on any sunny weekend. Venice—a former dream city of canals, gondolas, and amusement halls—jealously withholds from developers its strip of fine beach and fishing pier.

More miles of "perfect" sand reach along the lower rim of Santa Monica Bay from El Segundo to Redondo Beach, abutting the Palos Verdes Peninsula, an east-west belt of natural landscape.

Lower Newport Bay provides a water-oriented life style, and the Laguna shore has a lively, Rivieralike quality. By contrast, San Clemente, Dana Point, and Capistrano Beach are quiet settlements.

Angeles

...Work, a Passion for Play

Here build your homes for good,
    establish here, these areas entire,
    lands of the Western shore . . .
At last the New arriving, assuming,
    taking possession,
A swarming and busy race settling
    and organizing everywhere. . . .
                    —Walt Whitman

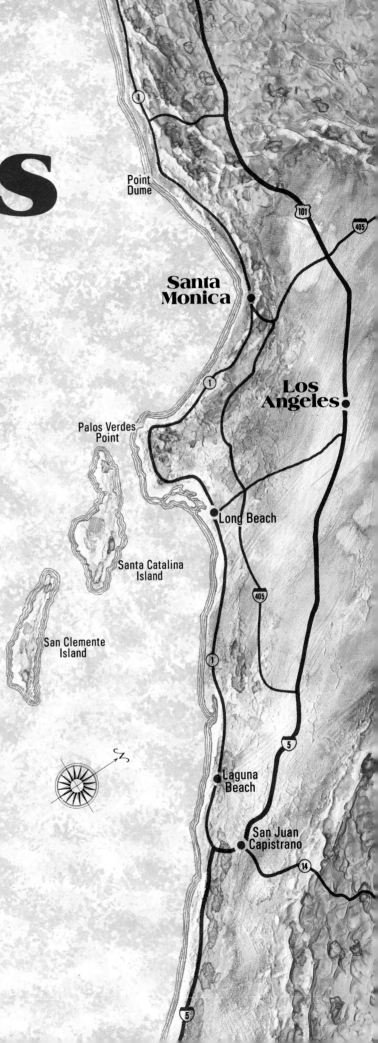

J.R. EYERMAN

*SOME OF THE MOST INTENSIVELY DEVELOPED
SHORE IN THE WORLD*

Tying together one town after another, the Los Angeles shoreline threads its narrow way along natural and manmade landscape. Largely undeveloped in the north (bottom of photo), the Santa Monica Mountains grade down to the popular Los Angeles Plain, and open seaside becomes increasingly close-packed as it skirts Santa Monica Bay southward (top of photo).

tatistics hint broadly at California's love affair with the ea: 85 percent of the population lives within 30 miles of ie ocean. Nowhere is this liaison more evident than on ie southern coast. From the lower edge of the Santa Ionica Mountains to Newport Bay, civilization iarches up to and sometimes over the waterfront. ompetition is fierce for waterfront real estate in the ensely settled, land-hungry southland. Only a law saved ublic access to the narrow strip of sand along the Ialibu shore. To the nearby population, the shore is nportant as a major recreation area. Every precious ich is used.

*SKYLINE AT
SANTA MONICA*

*Rock fishermen take their
ease while trying their luck
near Las Tunas State
Beach. Situated on high
bluffs overlooking the
ocean, the city of Santa
Monica has come close to
losing its touch with
the sea. In the early 1970s,
a startling proposal was
made to slice Santa Monica
Bay with an offshore
causeway topped with
high-rise apartments and a
freeway. The scheme
was shelved.*

Boomers and breakers, or the art of HANGING TEN

CAREFUL BEGINNING
Not yet a novice, a cautious tyro braces against the backwash, clutching his belly board. He's enthralled by antics of experts riding big combers farther out. Inland, an agile enthusiast manages to balance board, wetsuit, and himself all on two wheels.

In search of a long ride on the perfect wave, surfing aficionados flock to Southern California's shore, where the gently sloping sea floor manufactures just the right kind of wave, called "the spilling breaker."

Surfing first came to California from Hawaii in 1907, when the champion of Waikiki gave exhibitions at Redondo Beach. But apparently the sport didn't catch on until Hollywood imported Duke Kahanamoku to appear in films of the 1920s. In a matter of weeks, dozens of would-be imitators with backyard versions of his massive board appeared on the beach. Boards are incomparably better now (most of them are fiberglass), but because of their efficient shapes, challenging waves are harder to find.

FLYING FINISH
Hot-dogging it all the way to the beach, a single-minded surfer is oblivious to high-flying board of a wipeout victim who has been totally consumed in the sport.

Forty miles of SAND, forty million SUN seekers

What can you do on a Los Angeles beach? An urban-weary population in search of renewal finds both action and leisure there the year around. One estimate places the number of visitors at 40 million annually—a lot of square footage of sunburned skin. The beaches are family fun, havens for the young, an athlete's delight, and, in winter, a more or less solitary strand for quiet strollers. But it's the summer that finds the public beaches paved with languid bodies. The sea of humanity spills into the surf where the more restless have devised endless ways to play in the waves. For the die-hard beacher, activity continues late into the evening, with picnic fires blazing in concrete rings.

SOUTHLANDERS REALLY
USE THEIR SHORE
Most popular sector of the Los Angeles Coast—at least from the standpoint of numbers—is Santa Monica Beach State Park. Thousands of sun-worshipping surfers, swimmers, and picnickers are drawn to the beach on a bright summer day.

SUN FUN IS EASILY FOUND
Intense concentration furrows faces of volleyball players. Most popular beach sport, volleyball brings a dedicated breed to the shore shortly after sunrise and holds them there until dusk. Almost anywhere, one who loves the beach will find the perfect combination of sun and sea, above.

Marina Del Rey modestly calls itself the world's largest boat garage, and no one has challenged the claim. The manmade harbor comfortably accommodates up to 10,000 pleasure craft that sometimes all seem to be coming and going at once. Dredged from a salt water lagoon that was once popular with duck hunters, the marina sits behind the dune barrier that separates it from Santa Monica Bay. It is maintained for public use by Los Angeles County, but private developers have transformed its shores into a Venice-like city by the sea. Shops, office buildings, marine services, and luxury condominiums only a few steps from the slips bring the stylish world to the boat owner's gangplank.

ANIMATION ON ALL LEVELS
As modern as today, a pair of sloops tack spiritedly down the channel, slipping past old schooners and a square-rigged bark dozing at Fisherman's Village moorings, right. Below: Small craft fuss around a multi-lane launch ramp, just a stone's throw from a soaring multi-story office building.

Luxury, LEISURE, and a watery way of LIFE

TIDES
are giant waves

The tug of moon and sun on the sea creates a halfway world. In the narrow ribbon between high and low tides, a diverse array of creatures lives a rigorous in-and-out-again existence. Barnacles and periwinkle snails need only intermittent splashes; varieties of anemones and stars are completely covered except during the lowest tides. The species living in tidepools—the harshest environment—fall somewhere in between in their need for water.

Buffeting waves, evaporation, and fresh water brought by heavy rains are a few of the threats to life in this mid-zone. But the greatest of dangers is man's inquisitiveness and acquisitiveness. Every rock shields a rich variety of living things, and collectors who move stones or take home specimens are hastening the demise of intertidal life. The best policy is a self-imposed one: look and enjoy, but don't remove.

ONE ON THE ROCKS
Stepping from one slippery spot to another, an intrepid explorer scans rocky inlets exposed during lowest tide of the year. Canvas sneakers are ideal footwear for such excursions; they grip well and dry readily after a sloshing.

THREE IN THE SHALLOWS
Dwelling in pools that drain to dampness on ebb tide is a varied community of highly adapted animals. Starfish (top) wrap sucker-lined arms around clams and force the shellfish open by a constant pull, then extend their stomach into shell to digest its contents. Tentacles of flowerlike anemones (center) capture food that drifts or swims by, contracting when danger threatens. Urchins (bottom) feed on small organisms on sea floor and move by "walking" their spines.

*A CRAB IN THE HAND IS
WORTH TWO IN THE SAND*
*Though not hefty enough to
give a sizeable nip on a
finger, sand crabs can
startle an unsuspecting
sand castle engineer by
suddenly scuttling over a
digging hand. Lying just
below the surface of the
wave-washed beach
with their eye stalks thrust
above into the water, sand
crabs wait patiently for tides
and currents to bring food
particles their way.*

BOB ISAACS

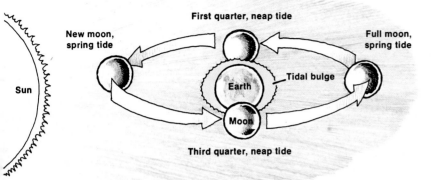

Regular rise and fall of ocean waters is caused by gravitational pull of moon and by centrifugal force of spinning earth. When earth, moon, and sun are in a line—as at new and full moon—force is greatest, causing spring tides (spring refers not to season but to "springing up" of the waters). Neap (or nipped) tides occur when sun and moon exert force at right angles to one another.

BILL BEEBE

YES, VIRGINIA, THERE REALLY IS A GRUNION *It sounds like a gag, but in Southern California, stalking fish with a flashlight is a pastime rather than a practical joke. During highest spring and summer tides, silver sided Leuresthes tenuis (commonly known as grunion) wriggle ashore to spawn. Fertilized eggs remain above subsequent low tides until uncovered by the next high tide, when the hatchlings wash out to deeper waters.*

Palos Verdes: Shoreside Refuge for the Urban-Weary

The City of the Angels reaches out for land, but in one coastal area the relentless march of development has been held back by a buffer of natural beauty.

The peninsula of Palos Verdes, which means "green trees," is the last vestige of the vast Rancho de Palo Verdes that remains true to its name. Once an island, now an arm of land that thrusts its rocky fist between the flat sand beaches of Santa Monica Bay and the harbor of Los Angeles, Palos Verdes has been protected by its residents from the dense development that pushes hard against its inland flank. Some areas are officially preserved as parks and state beaches, but many of the coves and bights below steep bluffs remain unspoiled because of their relative isolation.

The truce with civilization is not altogether perfect. Spectacular scenery of the cliff-top drive and the educational entertainment offered by Marineland of the Pacific draw thousands of visitors to the peninsula, a fact sometimes decried by its permanent population. Offshore, a sewer outfall has destroyed the once-giant kelp beds. Nonetheless, residents still regard their wooded hills as the only sanctuary of natural seaside beauty that has not succumbed to the sprawling city.

LEAVING THE LANDSCAPE ALONE
Facing page: Brush and free-growing grasses blend red tile roofs and whitewashed walls of a Mediterranean-style structure fronting on Malaga Cove. Above: A solitary figure finds serenity in contemplating the open sea from a grassy knoll. Nearby sign is a gentle reminder that shoreline is a protected area.

THIS IS A LIVING MARINE PRESERVE
PLEASE HELP US PRESERVE IT

- Taking of most tidal invertebrates forbidden (C.A.C. Title 14 Sec. 51).
- Always return tide pool animals to their original habitat after studying them.
- Please take nothing from the preserve. All animals, algae, shells, etc., should be left in place.
- Return rocks to their original position after you have finished observing their undersides.
- Carry no glass or other containers with you into the marine preserve.
- Practice conservation—it is a good habit to acquire. Carry all of your litter back to a trash can.

Palos Verdes Estates Shoreline Preserve

SEAWARD, AN OCEAN-GOING OUTLOOK
Getting to the waters that lap the Palos Verdes shore sometimes requires the agility of a mountain goat, but determined skindivers and surfers make it down to Lunada Bay, above, even carrying a full complement of equipment. Glass walls and redwood beams of Wayfarer's Chapel, right, harmonize perfectly with setting of cedar, pine, and eucalyptus. The peaceful place of meditation looks over busy Marineland of the Pacific to the ocean.

INLAND, A PARCEL OF THE NATURAL WORLD Early-morning sun streaming through a thin haze brightens commuters' route as they roll downhill, in no hurry to join with hustle and noise of another working day. Claims one Palos Verdes resident: "There may be a great many homes up here, but this is the only place around Los Angeles where there's some natural world left near the ocean . . . I hate to leave it even for a few hours."

With strollers or sitters,
PUBLIC PIERS
are popular

Public piers abound in the southland. More than in the north, they jut from almost every beach as one way of extending well-used recreation areas. Those who most value these boardwalks on stilts are either confirmed anglers or chronic strollers. The former aren't fussy about niceties. Their contentment lies in having enough water to wet a line. The latter take their pleasure in sniffing the sea air, browsing among whatever concessions may be available (though even these are secondary to sunshine and salt breezes), and occasionally passing the time of day with others of their ilk—including fishermen.

SOMETHING FOR EVERYBODY
Last light of day is shared by steadfast anglers and never-say-die surfers at Manhattan Beach, above. Mutual respect prevents encounters between lines and boards. A strollers' utopia, shops and restaurants of lively Redondo State Beach spread along the shore, covering not one but two popular piers, right.

Day after day, addicts of pier fishing return to the same spot, ever cheerful, ever contented, caring little if they catch anything. "Sometimes I don't even bait the hook..." confided a Newport angler, below. "I get my fun just sitting here." Coin-operated binoculars regard such frivolities with drooping eyes.

OUTWARD BOUND
Riding high in the water, a tanker rounds the bluff of Point Vicente and heads northward. Despite lonely look of the scene, shipping lanes in and out of Los Angeles and Long Beach Harbors are among world's busiest, and traffic day or night is heavy.

TWIN PORTS that are tops in TONNAGE

The quantitative data are impressive. Nine miles of breakwater embrace San Pedro Bay (see map on page 170), cordoning off the colossal complex of the Ports of Los Angeles and Long Beach. Fifty miles of waterfront are a panorama of clamorous, sweating, perpetual motion. In 1973-74 thousands of cargo ships loaded and unloaded millions of tons of goods valued at billions of dollars. Shipyards build and maintain craft of every kind, from outboard motorboats to supertankers. Fishing boats market their catch to the seafood canning industry, which is also based here. All this, plus a waterfront recreation area and the mammoth *Queen Mary*—now a floating museum and hotel—compete for one's attention almost as fiercely as the two ports vie with each other.

AN ENERGETIC, INDUSTRIAL WORLD

Riding low in the water, a trawler hustles to dock while crewmen secure the working gear and make ready for offloading operation. High and dry freighter in background is drydocked for repairs.

A WIDE, WATERY WORLD . . .
Located at western end of San Pedro Bay,
the vast Port of Los Angeles comprises over
7,000 acres of land and water. In photo, a
containerized ship heads up the main
channel, passing quarantine station at the
tip of Terminal Island.

PORT OF LOS ANGELES

TAKE A TRIP TO SEE

Moored permanently at the end of the Long Beach Freeway—after being retired from active service in 1967—the stately Queen Mary offers everyone an opportunity to step aboard a luxury liner. The monarch of the Atlantic is now an enormous maritime museum that includes Jacques Cousteau's Living Sea exhibit. Below: "Passengers" inspect a gleaming array of controls on ship's bridge.

Discovering
the SQUISHY world
of the MARSHLAND

Marshes, lagoons, sloughs, and estuaries hide great wealth in their muddy expanses. Their waters serve as a spawning ground and nursery for large numbers of ocean fish, shellfish, crabs, and shrimp. Their bogs harbor thousands of migratory birds. Their plants manufacture large quantities of oxygen. Too often oblivious to such treasures, man seeks to exploit the "unproductive" space of wetlands—to fill them, dam them, dredge them, drain them.

Only 125,000 acres of wetlands remain in the state, down over half from the turn of the century. Along the north coast, many marshes exist virtually in a primitive condition simply because of a relatively light population. In Southern California, though, where the pressure to claim new land is greater, 75 percent of the wetlands have been destroyed. The trend has been slowed but not halted. Thanks to increasing public awareness, several coastal wetlands have been saved from subdivision by being made state wildlife preserves.

UNDERSTANDING AN ESTUARY

Except for indomitable fishermen, few people love wetlands at first sight. The somber beauty takes time to appreciate, and the soggy underfooting does little in the way of extending an invitation. However, when estuaries, marshes, and tidal flats are viewed as a living resource, they are seen in a different light.

HARVEY HALVORSON

WETLANDS ARE NOT WASTELANDS
Most coastal estuaries go unnoticed by the traveler who is bent on getting somewhere and who sees them as unfit for human habitation. But those backwaters that have escaped silting and road fill are incredibly productive places that are home to innumerable creatures of sea and land.

Night heron   IAN TAIT

Blue heron   TOM MYERS

Belted kingfisher   TOM MYERS

173

THE BIG, WHITE STEAMER
It's a twenty-minute flight by amphibious airliner or a two-hour sea voyage by steamer, above. Backpackers have arranged for an overnight stay inland; casual sun worshippers, right, spend their day strolling the streets of bustling Avalon.

On a clear day you can see CATALINA

"Santa Catalina," crooned an old song, "island of romance." On a summer weekend, the island of romance is more like Coney Island. At least the square-mile town of Avalon seems that way as a steady procession of boats and seaplanes deposits yet another load of fun seekers. Once a sightseer is there, the biggest problem is deciding what to do.

Water lovers are enticed by swimming, boating, snorkeling, and scuba diving. Sport fishing craft are waiting for those who want to take up the challenge of topping tuna, marlin, and broadbill swordfish records. For passengers aboard the great, glass-bottomed sidewheelers, the unusually clear ocean allows detailed views of underwater gardens and intriguing sea creatures.

Landlubbers can turn away from the buzzing waterfront and tour part of the island's interior. Behind Avalon is primitive back country, property of the Santa Catalina Island Conservatory. A few roads loop the low, brown mountains; several riding and hiking trails drift off into the chaparral-covered slopes and canyons.

THE BIG, BUSY BAY
Though it's a "tropical" island—complete with waving palms and blue lagoons—Catalina is hardly a secret hideaway, especially during the busy summer sessions. Private craft jam Avalon Bay in such numbers that harbor patrol boats must do traffic duty.

GLENN CHRISTIANSEN

J.Y. BRYAN

*"IN ALL THE WORLD,
NO TRIP LIKE THIS"*

*Passengers debark on Avalon dock, luxury yachts
democratically bob at anchor next to outboards, and at
bay entrance a glass bottom sidewheeler settles down for
the night like a mother hen. Harbor view looking north to
Casino (actually a ballroom and movie theatre) has
changed little in half a century.*

"AT LEAST THEY'RE QUIET"

"...and if one starts to squeak, they just put a little oil on it...we've got plenty of that around here." Huntington Beach residents are not perturbed at having an idiotically nodding pump for a next-door neighbor, above. But petroleum can be annoying to beach users when it occasionally appears in sticky blobs that cling to bare feet.

LIVING in the considerable presence of PETROLEUM

The presence of oil is a foregone conclusion in Los Angeles. It has been since 1892, when wildcat prospector Edward L. Doheny tapped a bonanza that had derricks springing up from the downtown district to the surrounding hills. There are now over 9,000 producing wells in Los Angeles and Orange Counties.

In some places the industry has attempted to improve the appearance of the rigs by disguising drilling towers as office and apartment buildings, by hiding pumps underground, or by softening installations with landscaping. But because there are too many to camouflage, platforms and pumps sprout incongruously along beaches, in residential backyards, and in shopping districts. People have simply become accustomed to the sight—and to the pervasive smell on warm days. "That," said one Angeleno, sniffing the air, "smells like money."

ISLAND OF OIL
"Site unseen" oil platforms in Long Beach Harbor, below, are disguised as inhabited islands, complete with high-rise buildings covering drilling towers. From north of Seal Beach to south of Huntington Beach, the coast highway threads through an eerie thicket of stark derricks and uncovered pumps, above.

Helping hands haul the flat-bottomed boats from the surf, and umbrellas bloom as the beach by the Newport Pier becomes an open-air fish market. Its proprietors are the masters of a dozen 15½-foot dories, the last fishing fleet of its kind in the United States. Fishing methods were adopted from the New England cod fisherman. Early morning finds the doryman 10 miles off the coast, deftly paying out trawl lines coiled in a wooden keg and praying for luck. Then, laboriously cranking on a hand winch, he hauls his catch aboard and heads for home. As buyers eagerly call orders for the favored red rockfish or an occasional lobster, the job of baiting hooks for the next day's run begins again.

FRESH FILLETS TO ORDER
The day's fishing is completed by late morning, and market is set up at the foot of Newport Pier. A plank cutting board across a boat's stern, a scale hung on an oar stuck in the sand, and business begins as the doryman cleans and cuts up the catch any way the customer wants.

NEW ENGLAND
in Newport, home of the
DORY fishermen

A HARD DAY IS HALF-DONE — An outboard motor drives the Gloucester dories through the surf, and muscle power pushes them over rollers to the marketplace far up the beach. The first boat of the day to pass the far end of Newport Pier traditionally gets "first spot," a favored selling site nearest the street.

Pacific
WAVES –
packages of
POWER

ACTIVE ARCHITECT OF THE COASTLINE
Given birth a thousand miles or more at sea,
waves slide through the water as on a
frictionless conveyor. Expending their
massive energies against the headlands and
beaches, they cut away promontories and
move tons of sand back and forth.

The broad, unobstructed expanse of the Pacific Ocean spawns waves far more powerful than their Atlantic counterparts. Unceasingly they break in a rhythmic beat of surf that begins where the sea floor shallows. The way waves approach the land tells much about the offshore topography. Several lines of breakers indicate parallel sand bars; lower and higher areas of waves point out troughs and ridges in the bottom; waves that rise and collapse suddenly signal a steep slope.

The placid waves of summer gradually pick up sand from submerged bars to extend the beachfront, only to have it stripped away and returned to the bars by the violent waves of a winter storm. Responding to far off cataclysms, the ocean can rear up in tidal waves. But waves can also touch the shore with a gentle hand, sculpting fingerlike cusps in the sand and leaving the beach patterned with delicate ripples and rills.

**CUTTING AND WEATHERING—
AGENTS OF EROSION**
*Sea stacks, right, are created when erosion
and wave action join forces to wear away
softer portions of a terraced coast, leaving
arches (see page 131) whose tops eventually
collapse. Like a horizontal saw, waves cut
into the land, chewing holes in cliff faces,
creating caves and tunnels, below, and
polishing rough rocks into smooth cobbles.*

Where a beach has a gradual upward slope—as on most Southern California strands—waves roll in, retaining a smooth, rounded crest until their inshore end overbalances and spills down the advancing face, producing a curling front. Rocky shores (pages 182-183) cause waves to break apart in violent explosions of water and air.

THE STUFF
THAT SURFERS SEEK

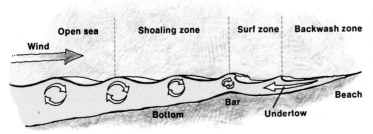

WHAT MAKES WAVES?

Most waves are caused by wind pushing the surface of the open sea into wrinkles. The water moves up and down with passage of a parcel of energy whose path forms a circular orbit (shown by curved arrows). In the shoaling zone, bottom friction slows a wave until its height and steepness increase to the extent that it breaks forward, creating surf. Undertow is the seaward return of water under the backwash.

BOATING
is the name of
the GAME

From Long Beach to Laguna Beach, pleasure boating is big business. More than a dozen major fiberglass boat builders and numerous smaller ones cluster in the area, making it the small boat capital of the nation. They sell to a populace that eagerly takes to the water in craft ranging from skitterish racing dinghies to monumental motor cruisers, seeking yet another recreational escape and perhaps some measure of intermittent solitude on the rolling sea.

Each weekend the multitude weighs anchor for coastal waterways, and solitude becomes but a word. Luxury power yachts, more like second homes than boats, cast off from private docks for a harbor sortie or a trip to one of the channel islands (Catalina is an all-time favorite). Eight-foot Naples Sabots, the most numerous class in the region, bob like peanut shells around buoys in sheltered water, skippered by junior sailors and old salts whose knees sometimes stick up high above the gunnels. Offshore yachts hoist colorful spinnakers during regattas. Most local races center on Catalina; a few favorites end in Mexico. And every other Fourth of July, sleek ocean racers from several countries leave Long Beach for a quick ride on the trade winds to Hawaii.

HOME ON THE HARBOR
In the watery world of Newport Bay, a cabin cruiser nestles contentedly in its landscaped slip, above. Out in Lido Channel, right, sailing conditions are crowded, and a catamaran squeezes by a sloop.

FLYING CAT
With twin rudders tipped up for launching, a Hobie Cat knifes through surf at Laguna Beach on its way out to a different kind of action in the wind. Even the terminology of these boats is acrobatic. The deck is a "trampoline"; the balancing rigging is a "trapeze."

**A BEAUTIFUL
PEA-GREEN BOAT**
*Working to weather on a
reflective sea off Redondo
Beach, a close-hauled sloop
glides under smoggy skies
the color of split-pea soup.*

**WHERE HAVE ALL
THE SKIPPERS GONE?**

*Looking like a school of
guppies, hundreds of
cruisers and sailboats sit
idly at their moorings in
Dana Point Marina. With
its artificial breakwaters
and manmade island, the
harbor is a far cry from the
way it must have looked
when seaman Henry Dana
viewed it from the brig
Pilgrim.*

For the SAFETY
of the southern
MARINER

During Spanish Colonial days, officials in San Diego hung a lantern from a stake at Ballast Point whenever a supply ship was due. But it wasn't until the mid-1800s that Southern California had its first lighthouses: welcoming lights at Point Loma in San Diego and Santa Barbara and a warning light at treacherous Point Conception. None of these three original lights is still in use. The Point Loma beacon, which was too often obscured by clouds on its lofty vantage point, was replaced by a skeleton tower at a lower level. In 1882 another lighthouse in Point Conception rose in place of the first, which had settled and cracked. In 1925 an earthquake finally toppled the Santa Barbara tower.

*NOT PICTURESQUE . . .
BUT FUNCTIONAL*

Constructed in 1913 and containing a lens that today is almost a hundred years old, Los Angeles light stands stolidly at the end of the long breakwater that protects Los Angeles Harbor. Automated light, fog signal, and radio beacon all are monitored from Long Beach.

CABLE CROSSING

U.S. COAST GUARD

**NOT FUNCTIONAL . . .
BUT PICTURESQUE**

Pioneer lighthouse at Point Fermin—built in 1874—looks across Los Angeles Harbor to distant mountains and across the sea to Catalina. Constructed of lumber and brick brought around the Horn, the Victorian building is now an historic monument, its lighthouse duty taken over by a beacon located at edge of nearby cliff.

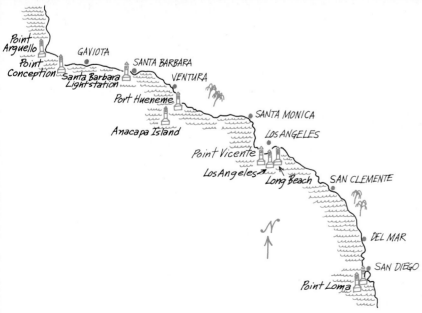

Point Arguello
GAVIOTA
Point Conception
SANTA BARBARA
Santa Barbara Lightstation
VENTURA
Port Hueneme
SANTA MONICA
Anacapa Island
LOS ANGELES
Point Vicente
Los Angeles
Long Beach
SAN CLEMENTE
DEL MAR
SAN DIEGO
Point Loma
N

LIGHTS IN THE NIGHT

Spotted from Point Arguello to San Diego, Southern California light stations are administered by Eleventh Coast Guard District, based at Long Beach. Many stations have radio beacons, in addition to a light and foghorn. Mariners who can't hear or see a station can take bearings of two radio beacons and discover where they are by locating point where lines intersect.

191

*THE OLD LIGHTHOUSE
AT POINT LOMA*
No longer active, the
spic-and-span lighthouse
atop Point Loma is a
museum of the life and
times of one of its keepers
—Captain Robert Israel—
who lived there with his
family. In the kitchen a table
is set for dinner, complete
with jam pot and toothpicks.
In children's room, toys
are scattered about as
if dropped but
a moment before.

THE "NEW" SAN DIEGO LIGHT

Because low clouds frequently obscured original beacon that was on higher ground, San Diego's light was moved to its present site at water's edge in 1891. Even when fog is thick, horizontal rays from a light —created by panels in the lens (see page 129)—can be seen by ships as flashes.

BLAIR STAPP

 193

DETOUR
to departed glory—
the CAPISTRANO MISSION

A continent away from the battlefields of the American Revolution, the declining empire of Spain, in its belated attempt to colonize the territory of Alta California, established the seventh in a chain of 21 missions—San Juan Capistrano. Through the years that the young nation to the east was pushing across the Great Plains, the missions also flourished. But in 1833 the government in Mexico ordered them secularized, and the resulting turmoil destroyed both Capistrano's prosperity and its very walls.

A few structures in the present surrounding town have tried to emulate the simple grace of the mission, which once was a complete city in itself, embracing nearly two acres of land. Preservation efforts at the mission have restored a serene elegance and a strong feeling of the past for anyone who will pause along the colonnades to contemplate the weathered, ivy-covered walls.

To Los Angeles

San Juan Capistrano

To Laguna Beach

Del Obispo

Camino Capistrano

N

Dana Point

Dana Pt. Harbor

Coast Highway

Capistrano Beach

To San Diego

To San Clemente

SIDETRIP TO OLD SPAIN
Only three miles from the Coast Highway, the village of San Juan Capistrano preserves colorful touches of its Spanish and Mexican heritage. Few are as harmonious or mellow as its venerable mission, founded in 1776 by Father Junipero Serra. Even on warm, visitor-busy days, the arcade surrounding the patio is quiet and cool.

AS RENOWNED AS THE SWALLOWS

Campanario is at end of a tranquil garden adjoining "Father Serra's church," the only remaining place where the founder of California's missions is known to have said Mass. A sign asks visitors not to ring ancient bells, which have become as widely celebrated as Capistrano's swallows.

San Diego's

The Sunny Coast—"...a littl

A word often used to sum up the character o
the San Diego shore is "diversified." Ye
words are elusive representations, especially
since this region diffuses a charm more
readily experienced than described
A sparkling climate blesses the San Diego
shore, helping to create an unusual combination of recreation and natural resource. Bu
climate is only part of the story. From the busy
beaches at the county's upper end to the un
developed Tijuana estuary, California's
southern shore is a pleasureable place fo
resident and visitor alike
At the top of this coastal segment, Camp
Pendleton forms a buffer against potential
encroachment by urbanization reaching ou
from Orange County. Though most of the
military base is inaccessible to the public, its
tenants—the Marine Corps—point with justifi-
able pride to their having instituted a nationally
acclaimed program of wildlife habitat
preservation.
Regional pride is expressed by most residents of the upper coastal communities. Even
those from other parts of California exhibit a
mutual concern for the area's valuable natural
resources.
In a travel-oriented society, La Jolla is an
oasis of another sort, working hard at not
attracting visitors. Farther south, tourism is the
reason for the remarkable Mission Bay Complex. And such commercial diversions as
offered by San Diego Bay fade to insignificance
in the sparse but natural coastal landscape near
the Mexican border.

Shore

"...more grace, a little more charm"

I have been to San Diego, a nice
little spot in the corner of the
United States where the climate
is delightful and Oranges, Lemons,
Figs, Olives, and all Semi-tropical
productions flourish....

—George Phillips Marston

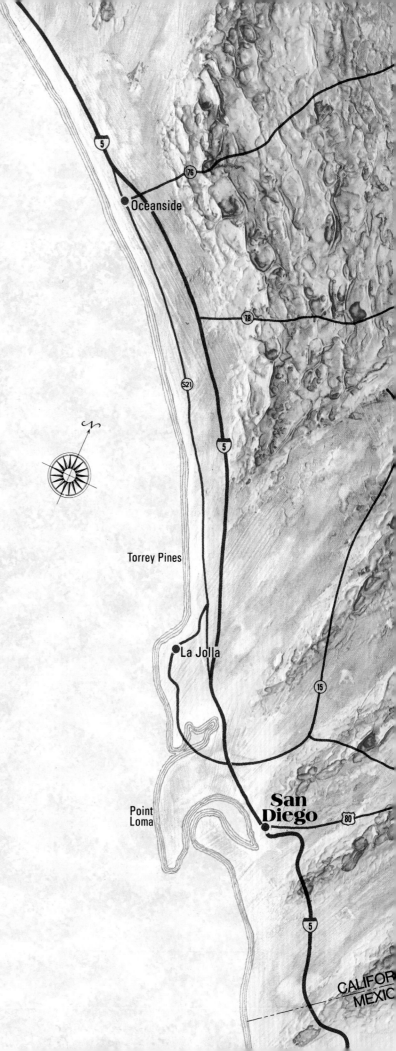

SUNNING KNOWS NO SEASON

On a sparkling day—and there are plenty of them for most of the year—sun worshippers sprout like weeds along the beaches. The sea is why people come to the north county coast, and the sea is why people keep coming back. Reveling in retirement in Leucadia, a native Arizonian declared: "People come over here from Riverside, San Bernardino, Los Angeles. It's the best beach area anywhere."

COMBING the county's north COAST

Unbroken miles of sand string together a series of sun-drenched coastside towns that dot the shore from the Orange County line almost to San Diego. Oceanside, Carlsbad, Leucadia, Encinitas, Cardiff by the Sea, Solana Beach, Del Mar—they are quiet communities, founded principally as resorts and now popular with retirees. An outsider cannot see a whit of difference between one township strand and another; his unjaundiced eye makes them all out to be equally captivating. But with wry regional pride, residents of each area claim superiority for their beach over those immediately to the north or south.

"Ours is better kept and less crowded," they say.

ENOUGH SUN FOR EVERYONE
Enjoying a whiz of a ride, a skate board enthusiast ends a long traverse down a street that is matter-of-factly interrupted by palm trees and a volley ball net at Encinitas' Moonlight Beach, left. Farther along the same shore, grotesquely eroded sandstone bluffs fascinate but hardly deter a determined stroller, above.

*SHORE OF
THE SUNDOWN SEA...* That's what writer T. H. Watkins calls California's coast. Morning
sun peeking over the Santa Margarita Mountains transforms the
sea at San Onofre to dancing liquid silver. But the shore's
evening mood is more meditative. Then, a golden haze
suffuses both land and sea, spreading a radiance that glows
long after the sun slips below the horizon.

DICK ROWAN

...WHERE THE TURF MEETS THE SURF
The San Diego shore is salubrious for both
man and beast. Every morning during eight
weeks of summer, sleek thoroughbreds run
the beaches and romp in the surf prior to
thrilling thousands of fans at famed
Del Mar track, opposite.

THOMAS MAHNKEN

FISSION
by the sea–the task
of taming the ATOM

DIABLO CANYON'S BIG DOME
Seven miles south of San Luis Obispo, Diablo Canyon nuclear power center offers a back-country bus tour to an overlook of plant site near water's edge, left. Diablo's visitor center features many fascinating exhibits that help clarify the concept of nuclear power. Right: Cranking keeps a panel of lights bright, but you'd have to keep at it for 13 hours to generate a penny's worth of electricity.

Nuclear power is nothing new along California's western edge. At Humboldt Bay, fission was put to work making electricity in 1963. Four years later the coast's second nuclear power station began production at San Onofre. A third facility at Diablo Canyon will go into operation once it's declared "earthquake proof."

Since these nuclear generators are cooled by an elaborate system that gulps in and spits out huge quantities of water, they are erected near the ocean. But the extreme pressure of water moving through a plant—and its temperature increase—can destroy indigenous marine life. Contention also festers about atomic energy's potential radiation hazards.

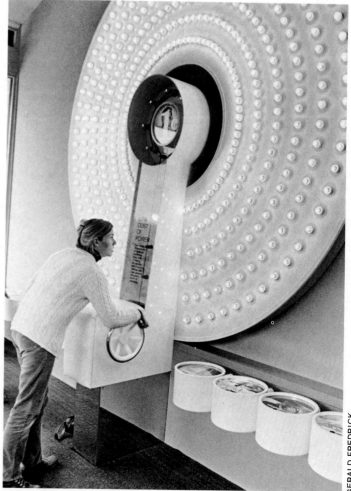

GERALD FREDRICK

Tennis ball dome that houses reactor of San Onofre generating station is familiar sight to motorists heading along State 5 south of San Clemente. San Onofre's first nuclear unit has a net generating capacity of 430 megawatts; two additional units increase capacity fivefold, producing enough electricity to supply a city of over two million people.

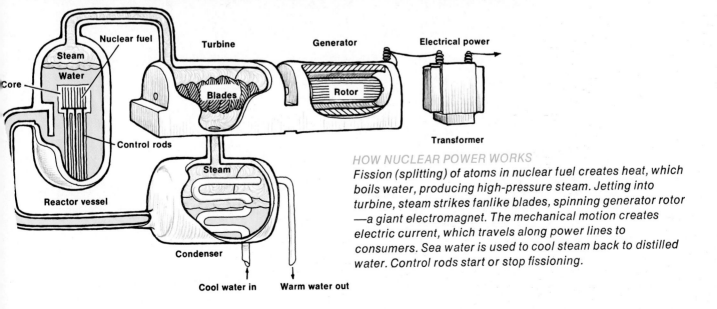

HOW NUCLEAR POWER WORKS

Fission (splitting) of atoms in nuclear fuel creates heat, which boils water, producing high-pressure steam. Jetting into turbine, steam strikes fanlike blades, spinning generator rotor —a giant electromagnet. The mechanical motion creates electric current, which travels along power lines to consumers. Sea water is used to cool steam back to distilled water. Control rods start or stop fissioning.

Torrey Pines: A Primitive Pocket of Unique Beauty

Protected from commercial developments and adapted to major geologic changes, a rare tree now fights only wind and drought.

The roots of the Torrey pine reach as deeply into the soil as they do into time. Clinging tenaciously to parched bluffs, the last stands of this rarest of pines grow on Santa Rosa Island and in a state reserve on the coast north of La Jolla.

In 1850 the fragile status of the trees was recognized by conservation-minded citizens. Efforts to preserve the Torrey pines were intense but followed a haphazard course until the final additions to the reserve were authorized in 1970. In the years between, the city council of San Diego leased the lands for grazing. Pines were cleared and burned for fuel, and fires swept the denuded areas. Tracts were sold to private owners, who began to draw up plans for development. This was stymied by the purchase of several hundred acres by the wealthy benefactress, Ellen B. Scripps, but a new danger had to be contended with: campers and picnickers chopping the trees for firewood. Housing subdivisions now abut the reserve boundaries where the race between developers and the Torrey pine's supporters ended. Although man cannot guarantee the trees' survival, he has at least left them an arena where they continue to battle against extinction.

A MONUMENT FASHIONED BY NATURE
Sunset gloriously illuminates the deeply eroded, 300-foot cliffs of Torrey Pines. Almost over the horizon, La Jolla gleams like a collection of polished pebbles. Sage, buckwheat, spice bush, and other native shrubs thrive among the pines and in the canyons; springtime sees the mesa brilliantly carpeted with wildflowers right out to the cliff edge.

...TORREY PINES

FAT MAN'S MISERY *Negotiable only by beanpole bodies, a tortuous path beginning at Red Butte worms its way between sandstone bluffs, in some places hardly more than a foot apart. Once you're into the passage, it's best to move right along without thinking of such things as falling rocks or earthquakes. Portions of the trail thread past exposed roots and twisted branches of the venerable Torrey Pine.*

CLIFF SAILER'S DELIGHT

Just beyond the southern terminus of Torrey Pines Reserve is a coastal stretch that is put to a number of good uses. At foot of cliffs—where the binoculars are pointed—is Black's Beach, a place of natural, nude exuberance. Centipede pier in middle distance belongs to Scripps Institution of Oceanography, marine laboratory for the University of California. Upsweeping sea breezes, deflected by the cliffs, create a midair mecca for sailplane and hang glider zealots. The varied ways of gliders are illustrated below.

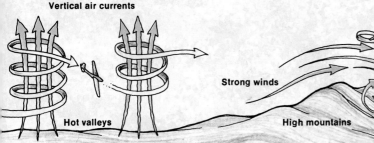

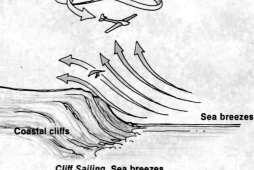

Vertical air currents

Hot valleys

Strong winds

High mountains

Coastal cliffs

Sea breezes

Thermal Riding. Vertical air currents, or updrafts, caused by uneven heating of ground by sun, permit long cross-country flights. Thermal riding is done mostly in inland valleys during the summer months.

Wave Soaring. Strong winds over mountain ranges form rolling turbulence in lee of high mountains. Some wave soaring is done along back of coastal range, but most is on east side of Sierra Nevada.

Cliff Sailing. Sea breezes flow up and over high coastside cliffs, making cushion of air currents for sailplanes, hang gliders (small object near cliff edge).

Pleasures and PAINS of coastside LIVING

What are some of the amenities that make people willing to pay the price of waterfront real estate? An unobstructed view of the sea's infinite faces; a feeling of living in close touch with nature; a breath of fresh air; a gentle climate given only occasionally to fits of temper; a handy playground. For all of these reasons and many more, the pleasure of having the ocean as a neighbor is a highly coveted one.

Unfortunately, a dream house by the sea can cause a few nightmares, too. Salt borne by spray coats windows and corrodes paint. Beach dwellers may wake up to find only an expanse of cobbles, the sand having been temporarily stripped by a storm. And the weather doesn't always live up to expectations. In spite of California's sunny reputation, there are bleak winter weeks of overcast or fog.

Perhaps the most serious problem of seaside living is erosion. Homes may be built on beaches that are naturally receding or that are being starved by such obstructions as dams and breakwaters. Clifftop homes may accelerate the already active processes that wear away their foundations. The simple factor of added weight may cause unstable bluffs to shift and crumble.

Lawn sprinkling adds excess ground water that percolates through the cliff and increases the risk of slumping. In some instances, water running off roofs has channeled in such a way as to carve ditches in the cliff face.

The answers to erosion for existing homes are sand hauls to replenish beaches, and seawalls or piles of broken rock at cliff bases. In the future, the ultimate solution may be to declare a buffer zone between civilization and sea.

WILL IT OR WON'T IT?
Celebrated for their sweeping seascapes—as well as their unstable bluffs—Santa Monica and neighboring Pacific Palisades sometimes pay for their proximity to the ocean. Supersaturated ground material—created by irrigation— and torrential rains cause large chunks of earth to drop away, not infrequently carrying sizeable portions of once horizontal real estate down to the Coast Highway.

THE ENCROACHING OCEAN

Paved highway once ran all along the Princeton shore, just south of San Francisco. The surging sea has taken great bites of the land, above, causing portions of two-lane to collapse and isolating slabs of asphalt atop crumbling stacks of soil. Left: Cliffs near Del Mar (San Diego County) are furrowed by water runoff and wave action. Without some kind of control, land slumping and sloughing off of bluff material will continue.

*LOOK . . . BUT
DON'T TOUCH*

*Momentarily oblivious to natural beauties, a
couple shares an intimate moment at the
surging sea near Goldfish Point, southern
boundary of San Diego-La Jolla Underwater
Park. The ecological reserve was established
to preserve the shoreline and underwater life
of La Jolla Canyon. Sea life may be
observed—but not disturbed.*

LA JOLLA is not the usual TOURIST place

The casual but refined feeling pervading La Jolla is wholly suited to the town's dual personality: it is strong in both recreation and research.

From its early days as a beach resort, La Jolla's atmosphere has been consciously maintained. Old shingled cottages still stand along the shaded streets, and most of the other buildings keep a low architectural profile. Good shops and restaurants abound. But the town has resisted such appeals to mass tourism as amusement parks, rows of hotels, and glittering night life.

Instead, La Jolla has gained world fame as a center for research. Scripps Institution of Oceanography is a leader in the field of marine study. A little north of Scripps rises the Salk Institute for Biological Studies, an interdisciplinary think tank named for the pioneer in polio vaccine.

Anyone coming for beach fun will find that La Jolla can match the best. From the quiet waters and intimate strand of La Jolla Cove to the celebrated surf of Windansea, the shore still beguiles with the same charm that induced early-century vacationers to linger here.

THE COVE—STEADFAST SEASIDE SYMBOL

Sea beauty is the reason for everything else at La Jolla. Since 1866 visitors have been coming all the way from the east coast to enjoy the ocean and the shore. Condominium with an ocean outlook fronts on "the cove," area's most popular swimming and sunbathing spot.

A LIFEGUARD'S day is not always SUNNY

The lifeguards of the southland dispel the old stereotype of a sun-bronzed Apollo surrounded by a covey of admiring females. To be sure, lifeguards are conspicuously present (and often bronzed and handsome), but to the benefit of the multitudes that throng the shore, they are also active, efficient, and dedicated. Many guards are full-time professionals; all receive rigorous training in rescue and advanced first aid and even a few tips on maintaining good public relations.

Much of a lifeguard's day involves routine patrolling, locating strayed children, and treating assorted wounds and cuts. Lifeguards also perform cliff rescues, deliver babies, and give talks on beach safety and marine life to scout groups and schools. Summer Sundays keep them busiest, for then they most often dash into the surf to aid swimmers in distress.

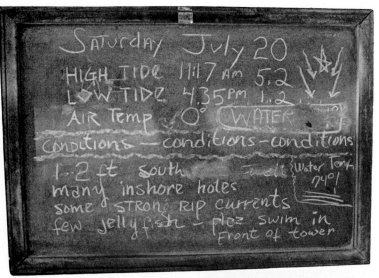

SIGN OF TIMES— AND TIDES

Updated frequently, a chalkboard at main lifeguard tower informs beach users of water conditions. To keep information current, guards periodically cruise the shore in jeeps containing rescue equipment and first-aid supplies. At some beaches, guards are authorized to issue citations to refractory visitors, though a spirit of public cooperation usually prevails.

WAVE WATCHING—WITH A PURPOSE *"Gentlemen, please move your surfboards to the south. You are now in a swimming area." In addition to safety, rescue, and policing duties, guards provide first-aid for cuts, bruises, jellyfish stings, stingray wounds. Main tower is linked by radio to Coast Guard, police, hospital, ambulance service. During summer season at heavily used beaches, some stations are manned 24 hours.*

SAN DIEGO'S
enduring bond with
the SEA

Less intense, more genteel, and more attuned to the tides than to the rush of progress, California's oldest city keeps a pace of its own. Surrounding the long, hooked bay that gave it birth, San Diego acknowledges that its lifeblood is still the sea. The Pacific Fleet makes its home in the exceptional harbor, and naval ships and installations are omnipresent. Enough ocean freighters call at commercial docks to make the city a respectable port, and close to a hundred oceanographic organizations find the location particularly suited to their research.

San Diego differs from many ports in that this city's waterfront is an inviting center. The Embarcadero is tidy, the water is clean, and the harbor has been planned for recreation as well as for business. The largest fishing fleet in the United States leaves from San Diego to seine for tuna as far south as Chile. Many Navy officers find the bay so to their liking that they retire in the town of Coronado on North Island.

Just north of the harbor is Mission Bay, a 4,600-acre aquatic playground where water activities are carefully orchestrated to fit simultaneously into a maze of manmade channels.

But to many visitors the city's best is still the grand old Hotel del Coronado. Thomas Edison himself supervised installation of the hotel's electric lighting in 1894. And since 1888 the rambling Victorian structure has hosted distinguished dignitaries from around the world. They come to enjoy the heritage of San Diego—the sea.

CENTURY-OLD SEADOG
Catching the sun with her figurehead and a Navy vessel with her stern, Star of India*—oldest merchantman afloat—is preserved as a historical relic on the waterfront.*

SEA . . . PLUS SHADES OF SPAIN
Facing page: Tile roofs and tower of St. Joseph Cathedral are a reminder of Spanish days of discovery, when—in 1769— the first link in chain of California missions was forged near San Diego Bay. Presence of numerous companies and institutions engaged in ocean research has given San Diego the name of oceanographic capital of the world.

...SAN DIEGO

LAY OF THE BAY

Finger-shaped bay is closed at lower end by thin neck of Silver Strand. The Navy is everywhere, from submarine pens and fueling depots on Point Loma to the Air Station on Coronado's North Island and the mothball fleet moored in the south bay.

SEAPORT CITY

As seen from Harbor Island, skyscrapers punctuate the city skyline at east edge of bay. Both Harbor Island and Shelter Island (see map) were built from material dredged from harbor bottom. Despite its heavy use, San Diego Bay is one of world's cleanest.

"A VERY GOOD AND ENCLOSED PORT" *Arriving on the day of St. Michael the Archangel, in 1542, Portuguese seafarer Juan Cabrillo named the bay San Miguel. Not until early 1600s was the discoverer's "good port" renamed—by Basque explorer Sebastian Vizcaino, who went ashore on what he thought was the feast day of St. Diego (he actually landed the day before). Discovery of California coast is credited to Cabrillo, whose statue stands at Point Loma.*

TWO WAYS
ON TWO BAYS

*Cat-rigged sailboats await rental use in a
stiff breeze at Mission Bay, above, an aquatic
wonderland featuring playgrounds, beaches,
golf courses, and Sea World, an enthralling
oceanarium. Concentration—not recreation
—is order of the day when San Diego's
far-ranging tuna fleet is in port, left. Net
mending goes on at foot of Broadway.*

VICTORIAN WOODEN WONDER

*Hotel del Coronado has hosted such
luminaries as Henry Ford, the Duke of
Windsor, Thomas Edison, and several United
States presidents. As it was at the turn of
the century, the grand old hostel is still "the
talk of the Western world."*

Coast WATCHING on a WHALE'S scale

Dispensing supportive enthusiasm in large measure, up-front whale watchers utilize binoculars, telescopes, camera lenses, and naked eyes to look for "spouts" of exhaled breath out at sea. During annual migration along the southern shore—from December through February—a favorite spotting site is the whale lookout station at the tip of Point Loma.

The Moby Dick parade, as Californians call the gray whale's southern migration, has shattered the aura of awesome mystery given all whales by Herman Melville's white leviathan. Plucked back from the brink of extinction through international protection, the grays range between the Arctic Ocean and the Gulf of California, but their obliging habit of sticking close to the California shore has made them a familiar part of the coastal scene.

From the moment they heave in sight on their annual journey, gray whales have precious little privacy. During winter months, thousands of binocular-eyed spectators follow their passage from choice vantages or board chartered craft that cruise alongside the docile 30- to 45-tonners. Scientists trail the gray giants to their breeding grounds, subjecting them to more intense scrutiny than any other species of whale receives.

"THERE SHE GOES!"

Flukes fling skyward as a gray whale heads for the depths. Surfacing to breathe, a whale blasts a 10 to 15-foot "blow" of warm, humid air. After inhaling, it sinks gently like a submarine, or—more dramatically—throws flukes, thrusting its wide tail fins into the air before sounding to a hundred feet. Some conservationists claim that whale-watching boats harass the creatures, causing them to follow a coastal route farther out to sea each year.

THE WAY OF WHALES

From summer feeding grounds in the Bering Strait region of the Arctic, the California gray whale swims a 6,000-mile route south to breeding and calving lagoons on Mexico's west coasts. San Diego Bay was once a calving grounds, but the whaling industry ended that.

POTPOURRI
...a California kaleidoscope

California's coast doesn't have a little of everything; it has a lot of everything—in tremendous variety. Weather? It varies from week-long fogs to month-long clear seasons. Wildlife? That ranges from sea lions to sea otters, from elk to eels. The shoreline is sandy, cobbled, sloping, precipitous, sometimes all in one place. You can fish; you can swim; you can surf, dive, sail —or just sit and enjoy. Offering something for everyone, California's coast is truly a kaleidoscope of pleasure.

Squid fisherman, San Pedro

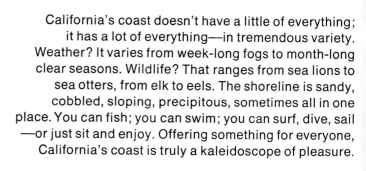

Lighthouse, Crescent City

Drying nets, Morro Bay

TED STRESHINSKY

Surf and gull, Monterey

Body surfers, Santa Monica

GERALD FREDRICK

Index